Gloria!

A Biography of Gloria Thurman, Missionary to Bangladesh

Barbara Joiner

WMU, SBC
Birmingham, Alabama

Bible verses are from *The Holy Bible*, King James Version.

WMU, SBC
P. O. Box 830010
Birmingham, Alabama 35283-0010

Third Printing

Dewey Decimal Classification: B
Subject Headings:
  THURMAN, GLORIA PHILPOT
  THURMAN, THOMAS EDWARD
  MISSIONS—BANGLADESH
  MISSIONARY BIOGRAPHY

ISBN: 1-56309-090-2
W934114•0200•2M5

Thanks—

To Betty and Randy Rains who dreamed that *Gloria!* should be and made it happen.

For all those who love Bangladesh and cared enough to send me there so the book would be authentic.

For all the people in Bangladesh who welcomed me and helped me prepare to write about Gloria's ministry.

For Jim and Betty McKinley, Jane Philpot, and Louise Davis who proofed the rough copy. They not only saved me from disgraceful errors, but they also loved and encouraged me.

For all those who prayed that "I would keep my sari up and my curry down" when I journeyed to Bangladesh and then prayed I'd keep my sanity and eyesight while I wrote *Gloria!*

For my wonderful, long suffering family—especially my husband, Homer, who ate more sandwiches than he's ever wanted in a lifetime, and for my granddaughter, Megan, who listened to most of the tapes with her "good" ears

Foreword

Imagine if you can, Michael Jordan or some other professional basketball player, riding a small burro. That's as close as I can come to describing my first image of Tom Thurman. He met the river ferry when I traveled to Bangladesh in 1975; tall, lanky Tom was proudly riding a very small motorbike. Another not-so-tall missionary colleague had outgrown the small machine. It was a vignette of the life-style practiced by Tom and Gloria Thurman. Tom used it joyfully, saving money for the Mission. For a long time, Tom and Gloria had no car of their own, choosing to use public transportation, crowded and uncomfortable as it was. It provided contact with the people, a chance to pass out tracts and talk to other passengers.

From the vigorous wave of Tom's welcome at the ferry to the more than gracious hospitality that is one of Gloria's most precious gifts, every contact with them deepened my appreciation of their commitment and heightened my love and admiration for them as my brother and sister in Christ.

Your understanding and enjoyment of this entire story, *Gloria!*, will be strengthened if you will permit me to enlarge the title in your mind to Gloria and Tom. She will like that, and we who read their story will understand that the music they make together is a duet of two superbly tuned instruments, both completely open to the direction of the divine Concert Master.

Let me give you the credentials for my evaluation—and praise—for *Gloria!* I spent several summers in Bangladesh during the 1970s. Bangladesh was a new country. After a bitter struggle for independence came a new degree of receptivity to the work of our missionaries. I returned in 1980, 1984, and 1985, each time learning more about Tom and Gloria and their productive thinking and working.

In 1960, I visited Trueman and Jane Moore in Dhaka, the capital of East Pakistan. Travel from Dhaka to Faridpur took 20 hours by rail and boat. By 1975, that 70-mile trip took a mere eight hours. I thought Faridpur was deep in "the boonies," but it was home to Tom and Gloria and their two sons. One afternoon, I saw their yard filled with more than 100 Bengalis patiently waiting for Gloria to "doctor" their stomach worms, open sores, and vitamin deficiencies. Nearby, Philip and David Thurman played soccer with the Bengali boys. There was no "us and them" attitude or isolation for the Thurmans, all four of them.

Gloria! provides a clear picture of the hospitality and ministering which flows constantly from the loving, Christlike natures of Tom and Gloria. They embody a fierce determination to lead Bengalis to learn about Jesus; the method they've chosen is based primarily on providing the opportunity for the Bengali people to read about Jesus in their extended family groups, or *baris*. The entire Mission in Bangladesh has been called on time and time again. The Thurmans, as well as other missionaries, give freely, constantly, and lovingly. However, the real priority is to call Bengalis to know the love of God through salvation by faith in Jesus Christ.

Read *Gloria!* carefully to realize what God has done through faithful missionaries in this field, considered so difficult. William Carey started work among the Bengalis—people who live around the Bay of Bengal—and Carey personally translated the entire Bible into Bengali. Carey started his work in India in 1793, the Bengali work perhaps ten years later. Nearly 200 years hence, we have the story of the Thurmans who have chosen to live their lives among the beautiful Bengalis in their beautiful but impoverished country.

Tom and Gloria left Faridpur in 1979 and moved to Gopalgonj, which I have located as 50 miles beyond the Great Commission. Although they are alone in Gopalgonj, they have worked with other missionaries throughout the years as a unique and dedicated team. One of Southern Baptists' most discouraging fields, by God's leadership and the faithfulness of truly dedicated missionaries, has become one of the most encouraging and challenging. To acknowledge the contributions of others—James and Guinevere Young, R T and Fran Buckley, Jim and Betty McKinley—is not to take away anything from Tom and Gloria. They are, have been, and always will be team players. They have been able, because of their spirit of cooperation and commitment, to keep the focus on the main thing—reaching others with the good news.

One other word: If I did not know Gloria Thurman and her work, I might be inclined to feel that a kindly author overdrew the picture here and there. After six long working trips to Bangladesh, 36 years of teaching missions at Southwestern Seminary, and visits to nearly all the countries where Southern Baptists have missionaries, I feel qualified to tell readers that understatement rather than exaggeration characterizes this story.

When a friend remarked to the wife of Theron Rankin that he was a great man, she gave a wise reply: "No, Theron is not a great man. He is an ordinary man, with the world in his heart." Theron Rankin is one of our Southern Baptist missions leaders who is accorded my continuing love and complete respect.

This tribute to Theron Rankin also fits Tom and Gloria Thurman. They are ordinary people, with the world in their hearts. They are my heroes; for them I have continuing love and complete respect.

Enjoy meeting them and knowing them as you read this book. Then ask the Lord if He calls the rest of us to minister with the same spirit of sacrificial obedience.

Cal Guy
Distinguished Professor of Missions, Emeritus
Southwestern Baptist Theological Seminary

Contents

It's Going to Be All Right

The doctor told the missionary to come to Dhaka a month before the due date of her first child. Gloria Thurman lived in Comilla, a five-hour drive from Dhaka with two ferry rides. There would be no quick dash to the hospital for Gloria and her husband Tom!

Two flights per week connected Comilla and Dhaka. The young couple planned ahead carefully. Gloria would fly in after Christmas. Tom would remain in Comilla until closer to delivery, but he would not risk missing the birth of their first child. The coming of the baby was the biggest event in the lives of the young couple since they had been appointed Southern Baptist missionaries to East Pakistan.

On the afternoon of January 5, 1967, Tom drove Gloria to the Comilla airport. She had an appointment with Dr. Hannah Klaus, a Roman Catholic Sister, the next day in the capital city of Dhaka.

Mavis Pate, a Southern Baptist missionary nurse, met Gloria at the airport. Gloria was to be her houseguest while awaiting the baby. Mavis had an appointment so she couldn't take Gloria for her appointment with the doctor. "That's no problem," said Gloria. "I can go in a baby taxi."

Literally thousands of the little three-wheeled motorized taxis swarm the city streets. Gloria laboriously climbed into one of Dhaka's finest. She remembers the ride: "We hit every pothole in the city. I felt shook-up from head to toe!"

The doctor examined her patient and declared, "Mrs. Thurman, I don't believe you will wait a whole month. Are you here in Dhaka to stay until the baby comes?" Gloria assured her that she was.

Gloria bounced on back to Mavis' apartment late in the afternoon. Around 7:30 that night she began having pains. When she informed her medically trained friend, Mavis replied, "It's probably just the jarring in the baby taxi. Don't worry about it; we'll do something to get your mind off it."

"I tried for nearly two hours to do something," recalls Gloria with a grimace, "but my mind was not taken off it!"

Around 9:30 she notified Mavis that the pain was increasing. Mavis examined Gloria and declared, "It's a first baby. Go on and go to bed and forget about this."

Obediently, Gloria climbed into bed. However, at 12:10 she cried out, "Mavis, I can't forget about this! Unless you want to do a home delivery, we'd better do something. We need to go now!"

All the way to the hospital, Gloria warned, "We're not going to make it! Are you ready to deliver this child?"

But they did make it, racing straight to the delivery room. Mavis knew the way and knew the Sisters, so they let her go right into the delivery room with Gloria.

"I can still see the little Bengali nurse," chuckles Gloria. "She was so short she had to stand on a stool to examine me. She took one look and cautioned, 'Don't bear down! Don't bear down! I'm calling the doctor right now!' She was waving her arms frantically in the air. She had not had a foreign maternity patient before. She was afraid something would go wrong and she'd be blamed for it. Mavis calmed her down and assured her that she was there to help."

Two Bengali women in labor were in the hospital at the same time that Gloria was. "I had never heard such groaning and moaning in all my life," Gloria says. "If I had stayed with them all night waiting for the baby, I would have been a raving maniac!"

Almost immediately, the doctor arrived and Philip Edward was born at 2:37 A.M. on January 7, 1967. Gloria did not have the aid of a single aspirin. Mavis recorded in her diary that she had never seen a first delivery so uncomplicated. Mavis also wrote that "her" baby weighed 7 pounds, 10 ounces, and was 22 inches in length. Gloria observed that he was a tall boy to start with and a good kicker. "He nearly kicked me to death before he made it into the world. I'm not surprised that soccer became his game," she added.

Mavis still had a big job to do that night: struggling with the telephone service to announce the news to Tom. At 4:00 A.M. she started calling. The Thurmans lived on the second floor of a big old house in Comilla. Since the ringing telephone didn't awaken Tom, the night guard rang the doorbell to make a louder noise. Tom ran downstairs, passed right by the telephone and opened the door. The guard said, "The telephone is ringing." Tom picked up the phone and Mavis chirped, "Good morning, Father Tom!"

Tom was shocked and embarrassed and ecstatic and disappointed. He had planned to be there! His young wife and new son were hours away and Tom could only imagine who the child looked like and how Gloria was feeling.

Philip did well. Gloria brought him home from the hospital after four days and they stayed with Mavis. Mavis fed him cereal at eight days. Gloria thought that most unusual. The Bengalis thought she was killing him. They feed their children nothing but breast milk for the first two years.

Tom arrived to see the fine boy as fast as their black Chevrolet pickup truck could make the trip. He brought along a little black box that fit right between the driver and passenger. "It looked like a little black coffin without a lid," Gloria recalls. "It also looked like it needed wheels!"

When Philip was only ten days old, the Thurmans tucked him in the little black box and left for Comilla. "I cringed as I thought of the long trip and two long, hot ferry rides. I was not my strongest just ten days after delivery," Gloria said. "Then I was immediately thankful that it was January, the most pleasant time of the year in our tropical country."

Gloria had every right to feel anxious. She was dreading bouncing on the rough roads to Comilla, and she remembered there were just a few Bengali doctors there if the baby got sick. The nearest missionary neighbors were two hours away in Feni, but the Thurmans wanted to go home.

God quieted the young woman's anxious heart. They were going to God's place of service for them. It was going to be all right.

The little family reached the first ferry. The slim, ash blond missionary slid out of the truck and smoothed down the long skirt of her pink floral shirtwaist dress. Almost immediately little Philip began to cry. Gloria picked him up and laid him on her shoulder and began patting his back.

"It's going to be all right; it's going to be all right," she soothed the baby. He settled down and closed his eyes again.

"I've often remembered that moment," Tom claims. "That's the story of our lives. Gloria has consoled each one of us and assured us that it's going to be all right. Whatever comes up, we'll manage. It's going to be all right."

Mother and child—Gloria with first son, Philip

Gully Dirt Poor in Rural Alabama

"Oh, God, if you will cause her to live, she will be yours," Nancy Philpot prayed as she looked at the premature baby. God heard the prayer offered for the baby born in the little south Alabama settlement of Caledonia, out from the sawmill community of McWilliams. He was to lay claim to that promise in a wonderful unfolding of His will. That baby would grow up to be Gloria Philpot Thurman.

Nancy Philpot remembers struggling from bed on April 4, 1941. She was extremely uncomfortable. As the day wore on, she reminded herself that her due date was at least six weeks away. Her husband, Bradford, had planned to go hunting that day. Nancy's mother, Amelia, wise soul that she was, insisted he stay home.

As dusk approached, Bradford set out on horseback to the nearest phone—four miles away—to call Dr. Thompson, the general practitioner. Dr. Thompson was 11 miles from the little farmhouse.

Meanwhile, Amelia walked a half-mile to the home of a cousin, Jerry Jones, to send him, on foot, a mile through the woods to fetch the local Granny Midwife, "Aunt" Ella Abrams. When "Aunt" Ella arrived, she and Amelia hurriedly prepared for the delivery. They gathered white sheets, boiled water, cleaned the table, and moved chairs to make plenty of "moving about" room for the doctor.

Dr. Thompson arrived just as Nancy's pains grew more intense. Around midnight, a 4-pound-6-ounce baby girl was delivered.

"I was a blue baby," Gloria says. "Mother said there was no circulation to speak of. That was when she prayed even harder and committed me to the Lord."

Nancy agrees. "Aunt" Ella and Dr. Thompson dipped Gloria first in cold water and then in warm water to begin circulation. Finally, after leaving her in the cold water for the longest time, he took her out, gave her a pop, and she cried.

"Nobody thought I'd keep on breathing," Gloria laughs, "but I haven't stopped yet!"

Gloria was the first child of Junious Bradford Philpot and Nancy Ann Hopkins Philpot. Two sisters, Mary Jane and Martha Sue, and brother William Bradford would follow.

Bradford worked driving trucks for either the sawmill or Wilcox County. The family farmed. They lived with Amelia Hopkins, Nancy's mother, on her old home place.

The community was small: the Hopkins place, the Philpot place (Bradford's parents) which was right across the road, and two other close-by neighbors. The next closest neighbors were a mile away. Playmates for the Philpot children were four black girls with whom they played and fought.

The Philpots were poor—"gully dirt" poor is the way Camden, Alabama author, Viola Goode Liddell, describes many of the rural people in her part of Alabama. The 1990 census lists eight counties in Alabama that rank among the 100 poorest counties in the United States. All eight of these counties are located in an area known as the Black Belt because of its rich soil. A century ago plantation agriculture dominated the region. It remains today largely rural with a predominantly black population. Greene County, with nearly half of its population living below the poverty line, is the state's poorest county. Running a close second is Wilcox County, the county of Caledonia, McWilliams, and Camden.

The Philpots may have been poor financially, but they were rich in love. Not only the love of Nancy and Bradford, but both sets of grandparents cared for them deeply. Living with Grandmother Amelia was a blessing. The children never knew Amelia's husband, Will Hopkins, who died before Gloria was born, but Amelia was a great encouragement to all the children.

Amelia was the one who taught Gloria to cook. "She'd let me stand in a chair and play in the biscuit dough and the tea cake dough. It's a wonder anybody ate anything!"

Amelia also did most of the doctoring of the children. The three sisters (Will was born much later) shared everything: red measles, then chicken pox, and finally, whooping cough. Amelia mashed garlic and honey and an unknown ingredient to make a remedy for whooping cough. If the children whooped, they got it. Gloria remembers running to the porch, holding onto a post, and covering her mouth so grandmother wouldn't hear her cough!

6

The girls tried not to complain with any problem, because Amelia's remedy for most illnesses was castor oil. Gloria swallows hard, "To this day, I don't even like to be around castor beans. I had my share of castor oil growing up."

Another favorite remedy was the hot poultice. "It's a wonder any of us have anything on our chests! If we hacked a little, we got tallow, Vick's salve, and mustard rubbed on us," Gloria shudders.

Gloria's favorite thing to do with her father was to hunt possum. Sister Jane was the dead-eye, however. She was a wonderful shot. Helping their father skin rabbits and squirrels was just part of the work on the farm. It didn't faze Gloria. She mastered skinning turtles at the side of Grandfather Philpot, as well.

Gloria remembers setting out potato draws, and bedding sweet potatoes when they were dug. She recalls going into the potato bank to bring out potatoes. She has longed for good Wilcox County mud to make a potato bank in Bangladesh so that she can enjoy sweet potatoes for more than one month a year.

She smacks her lips over the memory of good country molasses, then falls over laughing. "When we came in from school, Granddaddy Philpot would let us girls drive the wagon to the fields. The hands would load the sugar cane in the wagon and we'd take it to the mill. We'd unload it, and if we did it right, we'd be allowed to put the stalks through the grinder."

The children had been cautioned about playing around the mill. But one day, after the work was finished, a game of tag began. Gloria was given a little extra push and into the hole she went—the hole where the molasses skimmings had been thrown! "Tar Baby" had a time that night. Her long, braided hair was gummed together! "I've never been that sweet again in my whole life!" claims Gloria.

Cows had to be milked and fire wood split. The sisters fought most over splitting fire wood, over who was riding the cross-cut saw instead of pulling. Martha and Gloria always accused Jane of starting the argument. Then she'd stand on the sideline and referee while Martha and Gloria kept fussing and working.

Another chore that caused trouble was carrying water from the spring to fill wash pots and tubs. The sisters kept exact count of every single trip they made.

"We worked hard," Gloria recalls, "but everybody did. We got up early and worked steady. Except for Sunday: Sunday was the Lord's day. Caledonia had two struggling little churches. The Methodist met on the first and third Sundays. The Baptists met on the second and fourth. Our family went every Sunday."

Amelia and Nancy were Methodists, but the Philpots were Baptists. Right after Gloria was born, Nancy joined the Baptist church with Bradford. It didn't matter. They went to both churches.

One day a week, Amelia marched Gloria to the Methodist Church and taught her piano. Amelia played for the Methodist services and was training her replacement. "The little piano I know," Gloria explains, "I learned from grandmother. All I can play is hymns."

The children spent so much time with their grandparents because Nancy worked. For years she was a nurses' aid and desk clerk at Wilcox County Hospital. Even though Gloria never had any formal medical training, her training on the farm, and under Amelia and Nancy gave her a practical knowledge of "doctoring."

Martha tells of an incident that happened when she was just a child. A cousin had come to visit Grandmother and Grandfather Philpot. All of the children were at the Hopkins house playing. The cousin tried his skill at throwing an axe at the wood chopping block. Unfortunately for Martha, it did not stick in the block. It bounced off the block and hit her toe. In all of the excitement and horror of the moment, Gloria went into the house, got a clean white sock, repositioned Martha's toe and wrapped the sock around it to slow the bleeding and ultimately to save the toe.

Martha believes that this early training was equipping Gloria for her work in Bangladesh and she's right. All the skills, medical and non-medical, that Gloria mastered in rural Alabama would come in handy on the missions field. After all, "gully dirt" poor is a step up from poverty-stricken Bangladesh.

Reading, Writing, and Pineapple Sandwiches

Gloria thought she'd never be old enough to go to school. Finally, the day arrived and she boarded the bus with her tin lunch box. Inside was her favorite lunch—a pineapple sandwich, an appropriate treat for the eager first-grader. She traveled to Oak Hill's one-room schoolhouse to begin her formal education. She was such an apt student that she was sent to Pine Apple School the next year where she was double promoted to the third grade.

For the next six years, through the eighth grade, Gloria attended Pine Apple School. She and her sisters rode the school bus for three hours everyday going to and from school, and everyday the bus home stopped on Grandmother Philpot's side of the road. She always had tea cakes and a glass of milk waiting for each child. Then off they ran to Grandmother Amelia's to do chores and to study.

No fashion plate, Gloria wore dresses made by her mother from feed sacks and flour sacks. "That was another thing we sisters fought over: who got the prettiest sack for her dress! Besides, being big for my age, my dresses looked like sacks. When mother hung them up, you couldn't tell they had a waist," bemoans Gloria.

The dresses didn't embarrass Gloria, but shoes were another matter. In the fourth grade, teacher Gladys Knight took an interest in Gloria. Mrs. Knight always took time after lunch to read to her class; she read all sorts of stories, but always included a Bible story. Seeing Gloria's interest, Mrs. Knight taught her to use a flannelgraph. Gloria did flannelgraph stories for the younger classes several times. By the time she was a sixth grader, she could do a really good job.

One warm spring morning, Gloria was persuaded on the school bus to go to school barefoot. She had never gone to school without her shoes, but everybody else was barefoot that day. Her mother had said, "You are a big girl, Gloria. You ought to wear shoes." But she had not insisted that Gloria wear shoes. Gloria pranced in barefooted only to meet Mrs. Knight who beamed and told her she was to stay after school and do a flannelgraph story for PTA.

"I was mortified," Gloria recalls. "I begged my teacher to excuse me since I had no shoes that day."

"Well, you'll do it barefoot," pronounced Mrs. Knight.

Nobody ever had to tell her to wear her shoes to school again. It's an interesting memory for a missionary appointed to Bangladesh where she takes her shoes off to enter every house!

Gloria's eyes were opened to the wider world as Teacher Rosa Mae Sharpe taught her geography in the sixth grade. "She made me see beyond Wilcox County," Gloria states. "I enjoy sharing the world she taught me to see, when I'm home on furlough. It's a long way from Wilcox County to Bangladesh, and I never thought I'd travel around the world, but I knew there were people in far-off places and I wanted to help them."

About that same time, Gloria's heart was opened wider, too. As a 12-year-old she attended revival services at nearby Bear Creek Baptist Church. Brother E. W. Roark was the preacher. One of her favorite cousins, Mack McClurkin, made his profession of faith early in the revival week. Jane and Gloria rode with Brother Roark to visit one of their neighbors. They stopped at a cattle gate and Jane hopped out to open the gate. Brother Roark turned to Gloria in the back seat and said, "Mack accepted Christ as his Saviour last night. Have you made your decision?"

Gloria shook her head. "No, but I'm struggling with it."

Brother Roark nodded, "Well, the Lord will let you know when you are to respond."

That night as the service began, Gloria knew she had to respond. She hadn't talked with her parents, but she knew the Lord was speaking to her heart. She accepted Christ that night and came down the aisle as the choir sang, "Just as I Am." She and Mack were baptized together at Bear Creek Baptist Church.

School and church played important roles in Gloria's life. Surprisingly, so did stores. She laughs as she says, "Small stores in Bangladesh make me feel at home. I remember the small country store and gas station that was about two miles from home. There wasn't another store for four miles or so. That little store stocked everything from sewing needles to Popsicles."

Every Saturday the whole family listened for the horn that announced the arrival of the "rolling store," a popular traveling mercantile in the rural south. Everybody climbed into the truck and eagerly searched its shelves. "We always bought a block of ice for the ice box," Gloria recounts, "and sometimes I was given the money to buy my favorite treat: a garish pink, green, and white coconut bar called Streak of Lean."

Her fascination with stores continued as a 12-year-old. She rode with the rural mail carrier to Neenah, about ten miles from home. Gloria's great uncle owned a store at the train depot. Every Saturday, Gloria cleaned the store, put new merchandise on the shelves, and recorded purchases of those who bought on credit. At 3:30 in the afternoon, she left to ride back home with the mail carrier as he made his return trip.

The family moved to the Camden area, to Grampion Hills, when Gloria was a ninth-grader. She entered Wilcox County High School in Camden. When she graduated four years later, she had an *A* average and was salutatorian of the senior class.

From the time she was 16, she worked in the Yellow Front store. Thursday afternoon when the wholesale truck came in, she unpacked and put up the merchandise, just as she had at the little store in Neenah. Then she worked after school on Friday and all day Saturday. She began in the clothing department of the dry goods section; when she became a little older, she became a checker. "I remember my first payday. The check was for $4.76," Gloria chuckles. "I thought I was rich!"

Working at the Yellow Front, Gloria became more aware of black people and saw how they responded to kindness. When the older women came in to buy groceries, they nearly always ran short of money. Gloria would check their groceries one item at a time so that they could put back what their money wouldn't cover. "They responded with such favor," she remembers.

Gloria's mother worked in the hospital with blacks and had many close friends among them. She often said to her family that they were human beings who needed attention just as anybody does. She reminded the children that Wilcox County was 87 percent black and everybody needed to be friends. The example of seeing each individual as a person of worth—regardless of color or nationality or any other distinction—was established vividly for Gloria in her family home. An openness to blacks was not such a prevalent attitude in Alabama in the 1950s.

Gloria points to a particular time of spiritual growth in her life, when the family joined Enon Baptist Church near Camden. She recalls strong, nurturing leaders, like her Sunday School teacher, Mr.

11

Audie Davis. "I heard Mr. Audie say many times that God leads us one step at a time," Gloria says.

When she was 16, Gloria responded to an altar call. She felt God wanted to do something special with her life, but she didn't know what it was. In fact, when Mr. Audie asked her what God was calling her to do, she puzzled, "Mr. Audie, I don't know, but I do know I want to be open to His leadership, and I do want to do what He wants me to do. I want to go to college, but I don't know how that's going to work out."

He said, "You've heard me say it before and I will tell you again that God leads us one step at a time. You have made that one step. Now, God will show you the next step. You continue to seek Him, and we will continue to pray."

Mr. Audie continued to pray, as he promised. He wrote many notes to her as God opened the doors to college, as God led her to the missions field. The families continue to be close friends. Mr. Audie's death a few years ago was a significant loss for Gloria as well as many others.

As Mr. Audie had said, God did continue to lead. As a high school student, Gloria chose teaching as her profession. She prepared to be a teacher by volunteering to help first grade children read and supervising them on the playground.

"Helping those children and feeling their response helped me decide that teaching was for me." Gloria marvels, "God was preparing me even then for Bangladesh. Most of the work I've done that has really counted has been with children and youth. Most of the women, particularly in Gopalgonj, have little or no education. God's plan was falling into place even then."

Leacy Newell, Gloria's home economics teacher was her spiritual mentor in high school. She encouraged her and taught her; she helped Gloria see that she could go to college with a work scholarship. Mrs. Newell talked with a man from Camden at Troy State University who was in charge of student employment and arranged for a job for Gloria. Through her influence, Gloria received additional scholarship monies.

It was unheard of for a bank to loan a prospective student money for college. Yet a local banker lent Gloria money to be paid back when she finished her college work. So the doors to college opened for Gloria Philpot. God was leading; it was going to be all right.

Meanwhile in Mississippi

"My roots," brags Tom Thurman, "are in South Mississippi, where I was a barefoot boy in the 1930s and 1940s."

Thomas Edward Thurman was born to Javius (Jake) Thurman and his wife, Hilda Thomas Thurman, on April 13, 1933, on the family farm in the community of Arm, Mississippi. He was the Thurman's third child and the first son. Two sisters, Bettie and Louise, preceded him. After Tom came brother Dennie, sister Christa, and baby brother Jimmy.

"Dad said he made a total of $30 during 1933," Tom remembers. "It was the middle of the depression, and he was a farmer. Later on Dad became a carpenter."

According to sister Louise, Tom was a spoiled little rascal. She admits he was sick a lot, but she says that their maternal grandmother, Rosa Thomas, babied him. "He never had to pick up potatoes; he never had to do much of anything because a good wind would make him sick," she recounts. "Bettie and I were healthy as mules. We did the work and had to look after Thomas as well!"

Louise adds that Tom would beg Grandmother to let him play in the yard barefoot. When he came in from playing, she and Bettie had to take a washrag and clean his feet. "We hated doing that, and he knew it so he would deliberately stomp around in chicken droppings. We cleaned those precious little feet; he was a bad little boy!"

Tom doesn't remember that at all. In fact, he says all of them had a happy life. Jake and Hilda were professing Christians, but they were not regular in church attendance. Bettie, Louise, and Tom walked five miles on a gravel road every week to Sunday School. In the summer of 1945, all three of them were converted and they were baptized in July of that year.

They decided that what had happened to them ought to happen to everybody. So they began to work on their own family. They saw younger brothers, Dennie and Jimmy, and little sister, Christa, all come to know the Lord. Their father and, last of all, their mother came to a personal relationship with Jesus.

The summer of 1947 was a spiritual landmark in Tom's life. He had gone down to Magnolia, Mississippi, where his grandparents, John and Rosa Rushing, were dairy farmers, to work with them. Unexpectedly, Tom's dad arrived one Thursday in July, three weeks before Tom was due to return home. Jake came for Tom because a revival had begun at their home church, Arm Baptist, and he thought Tom needed to hear the revival preacher.

"We went back home, my dad and I, on Thursday," Tom tells. "On Friday night at the revival I made my commitment to serve the Lord. As far as I know, no other decision was made during that whole week. I often wondered what prompted Dad to come after me that day, but I do know a wonderful thing happened in my life because he did."

From that time on, Tom was known as the "preacher boy." The church took a real interest in him; he was the second young man to surrender to preach in 21 years in Arm Baptist Church. They prayed for him regularly and gave him added responsibility. He was elected Sunday School superintendent when he was only 16 years old.

"I didn't know what I was going to do," admits Tom, "but I had a wonderful pastor, Ray Pridgen. He told me if I was going to be a worker, I needed to be a trained worker. So I studied hard in school and graduated in 1951 from Monticello High School. I also started thinking about going to college."

Tom decided on Clarke Memorial College (now closed), a Baptist junior college in Newton, Mississippi. Arm Baptist Church invited him to preach his first sermon and paid him $50—his college entry fee for the fall semester of 1951.

Tom proudly explains, "I figured it up and my family helped me with clothes and a few other needs, but as for actual college expenses, I worked part-time and covered 86 percent of my college costs. I worked in the business office at Clarke, and later did the same at Mississippi College. There was a strong work ethic in my family. It was honorable to be busy. I just continued that in college."

In 1953, Tom transferred to Mississippi College where he majored in English and Latin with a minor in education. Numerous opportunities came his way to be involved in missions. He was in the Volunteer Mission Band. Twice a week the group taught Sunday

School at the Old Folks Home and witnessed at the Jackson city jail. During the summer of 1953, Tom served as a summer missionary with the Home Missions Board in Oklahoma. Later, while in seminary, he served as a summer missionary in California.

After graduating with a Bachelor of Arts degree from Mississippi College, Tom entered New Orleans Baptist Theological Seminary in the fall of 1955. The first campus Missionary Day was in October. Dr. Helen Falls, then professor of missions at the seminary, read a letter from Rex Ray, a Southern Baptist missionary who was retiring and leaving Korea. The letter opened Tom's eyes and challenged his heart. There was a strong appeal for new missionary recruits.

Dr. Ray said, "I have received a letter telling me that on December 1, 1955, I will be expected to close forever the doors of my missionary opportunities behind me. . . . I will be expected to climb down out of my little jeep. But to whom shall I hand the keys? Into whose hands shall I place my missionary Bible? Where are the young evangelists whom God is calling to give their lives of service in preaching the gospel of Jesus Christ to these multitudes who are yet walking in darkness to eternal death?"

Tom was haunted by Ray's words.

Baker James Cauthen, the president of the Foreign Mission Board, spoke on the next Missionary Day. Dr. Cauthen reminded the students that the places most of them would be going, at least ten others also wanted to go. Then Dr. Cauthen described a lost world where few wanted to go.

"I surrendered," Tom recounted. "That was for me." February 2, 1956, Thomas Thurman stepped out and made his decision public.

"I'd never thought of being a missionary before that day," Tom said. "I wasn't opposed to it; I just hadn't thought of myself as being a missionary, but from that day forward I knew God was calling me to the missions field."

In typical, thorough Thomas Thurman fashion, he got busy. He wrote his life history. He was completing his seminary training. He had already done a lot of student preaching. He had done some part-time pastoral work. He began talking to the Foreign Mission Board about the place of service.

"I felt a tug toward India," Tom related. "As a freshman at Clarke College, I had written a composition on Mahatma Ghandi which had a profound effect on me."

The Foreign Mission Board informed Tom that Southern Baptists were not then allowed in India. Would he consider India's next-door neighbor, East Pakistan?

Tom began to read and research East Pakistan. A special edition of *The Commission* focused on East Pakistan. The country was rural, dependent on agriculture; there was lots of village preaching. All that he learned about East Pakistan appealed to Tom. One major problem remained: Tom did not want to go alone.

He continued seminary and took a part-time pastorate in south Alabama at Enon Baptist Church in Atmore. When he graduated, he went to work full time. He was waiting for the Lord to send his partner in missions. Where was she? Of course, every grandma had a granddaughter who was a fine potential partner; it seemed every family had an eligible female. Lots of people wanted to match-mate.

"I had several little romances that never amounted to anything," Tom said. "I knew I would recognize the right woman when I found the one that God had for me."

College and Mosques and Minarets

Working 20 hours a week in the dining room kept Gloria busy while she attended Troy State University. For three years she kept a grueling schedule. During her senior year she became a mimeograph operator for the college. She really had come up in the world; she no longer had to get up early to serve eggs, and she didn't have to stay at night over mountains of dishes.

However, working in the kitchen introduced her to the international students. They had to work to go to college and their English was poor, so the kitchen was the assigned place for them. There were five boys, no girls, and all of them were from the Muslim world: Iraq, Iran, Turkey, and Pakistan. Gloria clicks off three that she came to know well, "Mahmud, Isak, and Omar."

At the end of her freshman year, she was elected international chairman of the Baptist Student Union. "It was because of my Muslim connections," laughs Gloria.

Her BSU director, Don Crapps, explained, "That means you can't go home for Thanksgiving. Alabama Woman's Missionary Union has a retreat at Thanksgiving at Shocco Baptist Assembly for international students. You will need to go with them."

Gloria went to the retreat for the next three Thanksgivings. "I began to understand their problems and feel their loneliness. They taught me some of their customs, and I began to share with them about the Lord," Gloria said.

God was leading, a step at a time. At the state BSU convention during her sophomore year, Gloria made a definite commitment to foreign missions. As she filled out the decision card, she noticed one question in particular: "Do you have any preference?" She answered, "I feel called to work with Muslims."

Gloria shakes her head, "God led me to Bangladesh which is 87 percent Muslim, and it all began in the kitchen at Troy State!"

At Troy State, Gloria was surrounded by wonderful vibrant Christians who nurtured her and helped her to grow. She joined Southside Baptist Church. An active youth program led by a fine layman, Junior Byrd, delighted her. Especially dear to her were her Training Union leaders, Mr. and Mrs. George Ledbetter. "I'd talk with them when I had a problem or needed guidance," she said. BSU was tremendously influential in her life. Director Don Crapps and his wife, Lyra, were the closest of friends. "I could always depend on them," remembers Gloria.

Walter and Voncell Harrell, a couple from Southside, "adopted" Gloria. Since her work schedule prevented going home on weekends she spent Sunday with the Harrell's. She went home with them from church and stayed until church that night. They lived within walking distance from the campus. If Gloria had a few free hours, she'd go over and work in their garden. Many times the working couple would come home to find the butterbeans picked or the tomatoes gathered and waiting on the back porch.

Another opportunity for Gloria was working with the BSU at the Alabama Baptist Children's Home in Troy. Every week she taught Bible classes there, where the long-awaited meeting took place!

Tom tells the story: "I was working hard down in Atmore waiting for *the* girl to come along. My seminary roommate, Roy Carter, was a pastor near Camden. He wrote to say that I needed to meet a young woman who was home from Troy State. This was about the middle of the summer, and I told him I was busy with Vacation Bible School and a coming revival. I would come as soon as I could get away. Well, I got there about the last of August and Gloria had already gone back to school. Roy took me by the hospital where Gloria's mother, Miss Nancy, worked. I fell in love with Miss Nancy before I even met Gloria!"

Gloria adds, "Roy Carter had told Tom I was a missions volunteer. So, after meeting my mother, he decided he wanted to meet me. He wrote me and asked when I would be home. I wrote back telling him my busy schedule."

Tom breaks in, "It was BSU this and BSU that. I thought I'd have to marry BSU just to get to meet Gloria. Besides, she was always cooking for Brotherhood breakfasts at Southside Baptist Church!"

By this time, Tom knew that Gloria was the same age of his baby sister, Christa, so he had some real doubts about their age difference. He decided he wanted to meet her anyway. When his church gathered the fall harvest for the Children's Home, he volunteered to bring the Enon Sunbeams and their two leaders to present the harvest. He worked it out with Gloria. He'd take everybody to the Children's Home and then he would come and get her at the dormitory and take her to the Home.

Gloria continues, "Tom came to my dorm and when I came down he stuck out his hand just like a preacher and introduced himself. We went over to the Children's Home where I also met the Sunbeams and their leaders. They knew what was happening and all claim to have had a part in the whole thing!"

"I loved Gloria that first day," Tom declares. "Within six weeks I was ready to get married, but I waited six months to propose. She was only a sophomore. She insisted on finishing college. I guess she had never heard that married women can go to college."

Gloria told Tom she couldn't marry him because she had heavy debts from her college education. Tom admits that he was afraid to ask how much she owed. She insisted that she had to finish college and then teach school to pay off those debts. Tom finally discovered that she would owe $400 at the end of her senior year. Nevertheless, Gloria continued to decline his offer of marriage.

Tom poured out his heart in a letter dated January 12, 1961.

Dearest Gloria,

It is a constant amazement at the hand of Providence leading and preparing one to learn and face the realities of life. Mr. Morgan, the missionary to China, prepared me for your letter which came this morning. For emphasis sake he told me twice, but I just passed that off as being the forgetfulness of an old man. Said he, "When you think of marriage, leave it in the hands of the Lord. He'll lead you in that as well as in everything. If we wait for Him, His will unfolds, sometimes slowly, but all the time surely." Thus, when I read your letter there was nothing else to do but to place it in His hands. Once again I asked that His will be done. In that spirit, I look forward to the future, though it is uncertain.

First of all, let me thank you for the frankness and maturity expressed. It was not easy for you, but your sincerity and honesty forced you to do it. About marriage, I have been quite frank with the Foreign Mission Board; it is with hesitation that single men are appointed, but on rare occasions, they do qualify. On purpose I talked with Miss Dawkins, now two years ago, and stated that I personally did not want to go as a single man. However, some experience in the pastorate has led me to see things in a different light.

All along, I have given myself until the fall of 1962 to find a mate; if one had not been found by that time, I would seek appointment alone. But even the thought of that sends a cold chill up my spine. And yet, one of the lessons of 1 Corinthians seems to be that some are called to this single life, so one's whole being could be given to the work of the ministry even as was Paul's. Though, I have felt that my most vital contribution could be made with a companion.

That too has its problems; since leaving college there have been three opportunities for marriage, I say this humbly; it sounds egotistical, but it has always proven to be the overriding of Providence. I'm sure that you, too, have had a number of opportunities had you made yourself available. In each of my cases, the factor has always been the call to the missions field. Not all of the girls were as frank as you (therefore, I say thank you again). All along I felt a feeling that the Lord was not in it. But it was not so with you. When Roy told me about you, I said that was the kind of girl I wanted to spend the rest of my life with. Then when I looked across the campus of the Children's Home, a bell rang and said, "There she is." My feelings have not changed from that hour except for the fact that a deepening of that love has come.

I made a decision in 1956 at which time I told the Lord He would have first place in my life. Even a wife would hold second place; it has been my dream that my companion would share in that dedication. Therefore, I could ask of you nothing other than for you to do as the Lord has given you directives. The foreign missions call is a difficult one; that call for a laborer on the white fields first was heard in the fall of 1951. I did not know until February 2, 1956, of the certainty of that call. I talked with all sorts of friends, counselors, missionaries, and pastors, but it was only the inner workings of the Spirit that showed me the way I ought to go. What I'm trying to say is, that there is no rush on my part. I shall pray that the assurance of His may be yours, either to go or to stay. To do otherwise, would be selfish and sinful.

Even at the best, the missions field is hard, disappointing, discouraging, but gloriously rewarding. Only those who have that "call" will be able to stay. It is a "call" that causes one to leave his own family, friends, and his own life. It is a call to selfless service; a call to burning out for God, out in a land when the workers are few; a call when each person does the work of five others—the Lord empowers for these extras. In short, it is a "call" where one can serve only as he is led of the Master. Therefore, Gloria, linger at His feet and He'll give you that direction. When you arise from that hour of soul searching, I shall be waiting for your answer. If it is a negative answer, dreams, hopes, goals will be shattered, but with the Lord's help, life will someday fall in place. If the answer is positive, joy of assurance will be the reward for waiting. Claim the promise of John 7:17: "If any man willeth, to know his will, he shall know."

Forgive me if I've caused you any special struggle. Forget me if I've but clouded the issue. But I shall always remember you as the sweetest girl in the whole, wide world. I'll admit I was too hasty, but when you find a jewel, you don't sit idly by and just look at it; rather, you start to work to make it yours. I shall not write until I hear from you. I shall be praying for you often and remember I shall always love you. In loneliness and expectancy, I shall be waiting. Pray for me. To the only one I ever loved, my Gloria,

Thomas

P.S. Gloria, about the financial ends, this will be a minor consideration, though it may seem a major one right now. If the Lord is in this, all the connected problems will work out. I can see a number of solutions. A married woman can always teach as well as a single one. After marriage, the Foreign Mission Board during the final proceedings, always allows about one year for marital adjustments. The least a minister could do would be to help repay a loan where his wife had borrowed the money. After all, she'll spend the rest of her life making his life happy. That is a mighty small return—a little money for such a glorious dividend. Don't consider that, right now.

She accepted.

She said yes!

Tom and Gloria look to their future.

Gloria
in Excelsis Deo

Gloria said, "Yes!"

Tom was the new associational missionary for Bethlehem Association in Frisco City, Alabama. He began his new job in May 1961. He put an engagement ring on Gloria's finger in October 1961. From that point on, every pastor, staff member, and acquaintance came into Tom's presence singing, "Gloooooooria in excelsis Deo!" It was all right with Tom. He was singing that a lot himself.

Tom and Gloria went to ask Gloria's father for permission to marry. Tom had a flowery speech prepared, but he took one look at Bradford, grabbed Gloria's hand with the ring on it, and asked, "You know what this means?"

Bradford replied, "Well, I knew there was a rat in the woodpile a long time ago."

Meeting Tom's family was next on the agenda. Gloria knew that Tom's mother, Hilda, was a very sick woman. She had Multiple Sclerosis in the advanced stages. Her one desire was to live to see Tom married. She worried about his going as a single man to the foreign missions field. She was not able to attend the wedding, but sent the whole family with her blessings. She died two months later.

Gloria recalls the trip to Mississippi. All the brothers and sisters, nieces and nephews, Jake and Hilda were gathered at the homeplace to see the girl Thomas was bringing home for Thanksgiving.

Just before Tom and Gloria arrived, brother Dennie roared into the yard. Everybody rushed out and swarmed his car. Dennie chastised them all, "Thomas is bringing this girl who has never been here and she'll think she's being attacked. What will she think of our family? Go back in the house and don't budge when they get here!"

When Tom and Gloria arrived, the silence was absolute. They walked into the front room where Hilda's bed was located. The children were lined up against the wall. Brothers and sisters were sitting everywhere. Every eye was focused on Gloria. "I would have run if I could have gotten by Tom but he was behind me in the doorway!" she promises.

Tom looked around in amazement, "I've never seen these children so calm before."

Dennie confessed, "I dared them to move because they just about took me down when I got here."

Gloria remembers that Tom's mother was the sweetest, kindest woman; Tom's family became Gloria's family from that moment on.

The feeling was mutual. Tom's sister, Louise, said that Tom had brought girls home before. Gloria was a different breed. "All of us fell in love with Gloria," Louise declares. "My mother thought so much of her, thought she was so fine, so right for Thomas."

Gloria was a senior when she accepted the engagement ring. She graduated in February and on April 6, 1962, Gloria Ann Philpot became Mrs. Thomas Edward Thurman in a lovely candlelight service at Enon Baptist Church in Camden.

"If numbers count, we were truly married," Gloria laughs. "There were 17 preachers at the wedding."

Tom breaks in, "Those were my preachers from my association! Roy Carter, who had masterminded the whole thing was the official preacher at the wedding. Billy Davis, my sister Louise's husband, was my best man. Jimmy Roling from Troy and Trent Rogers from Arm were groomsmen. Trent told me that he wouldn't kiss the bride, or she'd realize she had married the wrong man. Oh, yes, the younger brothers were the candlelighters: my brothers, Dennie and Jimmy, and Gloria's brother, Will."

Gloria continues, "My younger sister, Jane, was my maid of honor. Jane was in nursing school at Hale Memorial Hospital, on affiliation with the Providence School of Nursing of Mobile, Alabama, and we were afraid to the last that she wasn't going to get permission to come home. Well, she missed the rehearsal, but she did make it home for the wedding. My baby sister, Martha Sue, Tom's sister, Christa, and Linda Davis were bridesmaids."

Veteria Hester, Gloria's college roommate, was soloist and Flay Lowery, a very special college friend, was pianist.

"People were so kind to us," Gloria remembers. "Mrs. Becky Bonner, the former home economics teacher at Moore Academy in Pine Apple and a really good friend of my mother's, made our wedding cake as her gift to us. Another close friend of my mother's, Esther Allen, made my white satin dress. The women of the church planned the reception and provided everything. It was a beautiful wedding and reception.

Tom had hidden his car about eight miles from the church. All his preacher friends had been teasing him about what they were going to do. A trusted friend was to take them to his car, but other mischief was afoot. Jane, Audie Davis, Jr., and his sister, Linda, were not going to be stopped. They followed along after the reception. Audie had just finished medical school and Tom liked and respected him. When Audie offered to carry Gloria's bag to the car, Tom handed it to him. Of course, they took out half the stuff in the bag and then put it in the car. They followed the couple for 20 miles and then passed them. Flying from their radio aerial was one of Gloria's nylon slips. It embarrassed Gloria, but she claims she could see Tom blushing even in the dark!

The funniest event happened to Billy and Louise, however. Everybody thought the newlyweds would make their getaway in their big Oldsmobile. So it had been decorated to a fare-the-well. Billy drove his own car back to Mississippi that night. Halfway there he stopped for gas. The gas attendant peered into the car: it held Billy, Louise, their small baby, Tom's sister, both brothers, a groomsman, and Beulah, who had come to take care of the baby. When Billy paid for the gas, the attendant said, "Waited sort of late to get married, didn't you?"

Mr. and Mrs. Thomas Thurman honeymooned in Gatlinburg, Tennessee. "We really lived high," Gloria sighs "We had a nice little cabin right beside a stream. We took in the sights of Gatlinburg and feasted on wonderful meals."

On their way home, however, Tom confessed that he'd spent all of April's salary. The truth of the matter was Bethlehem Association was a small, struggling association which didn't have much money. The fine deacon who served as treasurer for the association always knew when the churches had not sent in their money. He would call Tom and say, "Come on down to the grocery store and get your groceries for the week. You can pay when your salary comes." Lots of times the check didn't come until the 15th or 16th of the month. The young couple learned to live on a shoestring, but both of them had always done that. Gloria stoutly maintains, "We've not wanted for anything and we've had a happy life."

They didn't want for much; when they returned home from their honeymoon the association gave them an enormous "pounding," stocking their pantry with pounds of flour and sugar and other food-stuffs. Tom and Gloria settled in upstairs in a big, old two-story house that Tom had been renting from the McKenzies in Frisco City. After a few months, a small house which also belonged to the McKenzies became available. The little house was home until Tom and Gloria left for East Pakistan.

Waiting for appointment, they had a full schedule. Gloria taught school to pay off her terrible debt! Tom taught January Bible studies; both did Home Mission and Foreign Mission Studies, and Vacation Bible Schools.

Their time of missionary appointment finally came in June 1964. The Thurmans were ready to go to the Muslim world.

Mrs. Tom Thurman

Overdue on My Visa

Appointment to East Pakistan came June 18, 1964. The Thurmans went to Richmond, Virginia, for orientation. They submitted their resignations, effective August 1, Tom to Bethlehem Baptist Association and Gloria to the school board. Then they waited—for 18 months. "God was teaching us patience," said Tom.

"We didn't have our own roof over our heads," Gloria bemoaned. "Of course, we didn't know we'd wait a year-and-a-half. Everyday we thought the visas would come through."

The couple stayed with Tom's family in Mississippi for two weeks, then traveled to Miss Nancy's in Alabama. The Foreign Mission Board would call to say it would take a month, then Tom and Gloria would go back to Mississippi. "We were nomads," Tom remarks.

During this interim, the Foreign Mission Board purchased a microbus for use in Indonesia. They wanted to send a used bus, so they asked Tom and Gloria to drive it until they left for East Pakistan. By the time they drove it to New Orleans to be shipped to Indonesia, they had logged 12,000 miles.

Before the Thurmans ever reached the missions field, Gloria was asked to go to a World Mission Conference. She worked hard to make East Pakistan real to the people attending. For 40 minutes she spoke from her heart about East Pakistan. She turned the service over to the pastor who stood and said, "I want us to pray for Sis and her man while they go . . . Where is it you're going, Sis?" It was not the last time that others failed to share Gloria's concern for the far-off world of East Pakistan.

During the long wait for visas, war broke out between Pakistan and India. Tom called Winston Crawley at the Foreign Mission Board. "I told him that maybe we had misunderstood God's will.

We were both so sure it was East Pakistan, but it looked as if we couldn't get a visa anytime soon. I told Dr. Crawley we were ready to talk about going somewhere else."

Dr. Crawley advised, "Let me check and I'll call you back in a day or two." When he called back he asked the Thurmans to pray about going temporarily to the Philippines to Clark Field to work with the English-speaking church or perhaps to Singapore.

Tom and Gloria thought about it and prayed.

A week later, Dr. Crawley called to report, "A very strange thing has happened. The Pakistani Embassy has your visas. Go to Singapore and wait six weeks. Give this conflict time to settle down, and then plan to go on to East Pakistan."

Gloria adds, "The conflict continued. It was the dispute over Kashmir, and China became involved. It didn't look good. The women and children in the East Pakistan Mission had been evacuated to the Philippines. We were in Singapore ready to go in!"

"We had a wonderful six weeks in Singapore," Tom continues. "In fact, we decided if the door closed to East Pakistan, we'd like very much to work in Singapore."

However, at the end of six weeks Tom and Gloria flew into East Pakistan. They arrived in Dhaka on December 7, 1965. The airport was surrounded by sandbags because they were expecting an attack from India. Immediately after their plane landed, all the lights on the runway and in the airport were turned off.

"We had to fill in two long pages of information," Gloria shudders. "I kept worrying about putting down the wrong thing."

"We had sent a telegram to our Baptist Mission to say that we were coming," Tom explains. "But nobody was there to meet us. We found out later that the telegram was never delivered."

As they struggled with the papers, Gloria spotted a man who looked like an American. He came over to the Thurmans and introduced himself as Paul Hutchinson, a Church of God missionary. He asked, "Does anyone know you are coming?"

Tom assured him that he'd sent a telegram.

The new friend called the Baptist Mission office. Missionary Trueman Moore was there and he came to pick up the Thurmans.

Gloria remembers, "In that dark airport, in a strange new land, we knew calm assurance: This is the place God has called us; this is the place we are to serve."

Trueman took them to the Mission Guest House, where they would stay for several months. "I've often said I started with a shock," laughs Gloria. "The first morning in the country, I got out of bed and was shocked when I touched a metal cabinet! I've continued in a state of shock for as long as I've been here."

After Tom and Gloria moved into their brand new Lottie Moon house, one of their first guests was Juliette Mather, an editor for WMU from 1921 until 1957. When they escorted Miss Mather to her bedroom, she asked for an umbrella. A leak was pouring water right on the bed—in their new house!

Miss Mather visited when Gloria was expecting Philip. She wanted to see Faridpur. At that time there were three ferries between Dhaka and Faridpur. The Mission driver took them to the first ferry; they were to continue on public buses. The ferry gate had already rolled up and the only way to get on the ferry was to go over the side. There was one step and then you just jumped over.

Gloria laughs, "Miss Mather held out her hands and the men helped her up. She was a petite, white-haired lady. Then I came along, six months pregnant. They didn't even try to help me up. I had to haul myself onto the ferry."

Tom and Gloria were deep into language study. Tom had taken time to write home two days after their arrival in Dhaka, requesting prayer: "Our first assignment will be language study, which is Bengali. English is spoken by some, but only a thorough knowledge of their language can break down many barriers. Please pray for us as we apply ourselves to this difficult task."

For seven months, Tom and Gloria studied in the Mission language school in Dhaka. Not long after they started, Mavis Pate, the single nurse in the Mission, returned from the Philippines and she, too, was a language student. Mavis was more advanced than the Thurmans. She had her own teacher; Tom and Gloria had their own teacher. They went to class from eight until noon. They'd study all afternoon and into the night to be ready for the next day.

"Our teachers were sympathetic; they knew why we were here. Most were Christians, and they overlooked many mistakes," Gloria explains. "Tom and one teacher had such love and respect for each other that the teacher simply would not correct him properly. Tom has suffered from that."

Gloria continues, "You have to know that the Bengalis love their language. They fought for the right to speak Bengali. The people in East Pakistan have always spoken Bengali. When the partition of India came in 1947 creating Pakistan, there were two sides of Pakistan: West Pakistan on the western side of India, and East Pakistan on the eastern side. People in West Pakistan spoke Urdu, and decreed that the official language of all Pakistan was Urdu.

People here fought to speak Bengali. They couldn't speak Urdu, didn't want to speak Urdu. The language movement came about and many people died, so they are fiercely proud of their language.

"Bengalis are pleased when foreigners speak their language, but they are quick to correct. Tom says they keep us humble!"

In August 1966, Tom and Gloria moved to Comilla, about 80 miles from Dhaka. In a letter home Tom shares, "Comilla is a five-hour trip by car because we have to cross two rivers on ferries."

In that same letter, he rejoiced that their "worldly goods," which had been in storage since 1964, finally made it to Dhaka!

In Comilla, Tom and Gloria continued language study, each with a private tutor who helped with the rest of their formal studies. Women are required to study two years, men for three. The third year is for religious terminology. Gloria decided to study the third year as well. Both took their examinations in June 1968 and passed. They left on their first furlough in September.

During those days in Comilla, Gloria also managed to have her first baby, Philip Edward.

The first term had been a learning term—not only the language, but the land as well. Tom wrote:

Ours is a fascinating land: We have seen:
Three cobras dancing to the tune of a bamboo flute.
Men and women carrying heavy loads on their heads,
Lush rice fields, and later the golden grain.
Riverboats on the land's many streams.
Women in their beautiful flowing saris.
Men with their bare backs and wrap-around skirts, called *lungis.*
The bazaar with its meats covered in thumbnail sized flies.
The drug store, with needles and syringes, unsterile, lying on the
    counter but ready for use.
Naked children busy with their play.
Mothers washing their dishes in the nearby stream in the same
    water where the family had bathed.

Ours is a needy land: We saw:
    A man beaten by an angry mob, while the police stood
    helplessly by.
Searching students looking for a better life.
Thousands of beggars, blind, lame, diseased.

Many more who are poverty-stricken in spirit because they do
   not know the Saviour's love.
Souls in sin who do not know that Christ has come."

In another letter, Tom tells of some things he and Gloria had
learned about being a missionary: "We have found that a missionary needs the patience of Job, the love of John, the wisdom of
Solomon, the meekness of David, the boldness of Peter, the call of
Isaiah, the faith of Abraham, the endurance of Jonah, the passion
of Jeremiah and the zeal of Paul. We feel that our first term has
been a 'boot camp.' The Lord has shown us the challenge of His
work. Daily we have thanked our blessed Lord that He opened the
door for us to serve here."

Eighteen months of waiting, thousands of new words, dozens of
new customs, countless ferry rides, untold surprises—it was all
worth it. Tom and Gloria had found a home in East Pakistan.

New missionaries, Tom and Gloria, with language teachers, Nicholas and Shova Rozario in Comilla.

Three Thurmans to Faridpur—No, Four!

The Thurmans had a wonderful furlough in Camden, Alabama, with Miss Nancy. They traveled and spoke and showed off their new baby, Philip. Many times they were asked, "Are you really going back to that faraway country?"

This was their answer:

> If you had been to heathen lands,
> Where weary ones with eager hands,
> Still plead, yet no one understands,
> Would you go back?
> > Would you?
> If you had seen them in despair,
> Beat on their breast,
> Pull out their hair,
> While demon powers fill the air,
> Would you go back?
> > Would you?
> If you had seen the glorious sight,
> When weary ones late at night,
> Are brought from darkness into light,
> Would you go back?
> > Would you?
> Yet they wait, a weary throng,
> They've waited some so very long.
> When shall darkness be turned to song,
> Would you go back?
> > Would you?

(poem copied; source unknown)

They went back in July 1969. The Baptist Mission asked them to go to Faridpur, three river ferries from Dhaka.

They moved into the Troy and Marjorie Bennett house, which had been the Carl and Jean Ryther house, so Tom and Gloria were following in missions history. The Bennetts and Rythers were long-time Southern Baptist missionaries in East Pakistan.

The house was on a compound; all of the neighbors were Christians. "It was a wonderful place to raise children," Gloria says. "It was also good for me as I became accustomed to the society and found what I could and could not do."

Four months after moving to Faridpur, Gloria made another planned trip to Dhaka. Tom went with her this time to Holy Family Hospital in Dhaka. Dr. Jeung, another Roman Catholic Sister, was Gloria's doctor this pregnancy. However, she was not as fast as Gloria and missed the birth completely.

"I don't know what women are talking about when they moan about all the stress and strain of childbirth, but Tom can sympathize with them!" Gloria smiled.

Mavis Pate and Gloria had tried to prepare Tom. He insisted that he was going to be present for the birth of his second child. Gloria had practiced deep breathing to prepare for natural childbirth so she knew what to do and had Mavis to encourage her.

When the time grew near, Mavis called Tom to the delivery room. Gloria was dealing with a bout of hard pains, gasping for breath, when she looked up at Tom. "The top of his head was pouring perspiration! I was afraid he was going to faint," remembers Gloria. "I told Mavis to take him for air."

Before Mavis could react, Tom gasped, "Mavis, you know what to do in here. I think I'd better get some air!"

Mavis and Gloria made it through for the second time; David Olive Thurman was born October 7, 1969, weighing seven pounds and two ounces. After Mavis cleaned up the newborn, Tom returned to greet his new son, greatly relieved that the ordeal was over.

Gloria and David left the hospital after two days. They stayed with "Aunt" Mavis in Dhaka, until making the hot trip to Faridpur when David was only ten days old.

Tom began his village outreach working with the local pastor. He had found his love. He would never be moved from working with people in the villages. Gloria found her love, too. She began working with the young girls in the Faridpur Baptist Church, helping them to learn hymns and memorize Scripture verses. She also taught them in Sunday School.

In addition, Gloria had two little boys to care for. Illnesses are frightening in the United States with well-trained doctors and excellent medical facilities. In Comilla and Faridpur, illnesses are terrifying and sometimes fatal. Philip developed bronchial asthma. Many nights in Comilla, Tom and Gloria sat up all night holding the child and rocking him. Even if they propped him up, he could not sleep because his breathing would almost stop.

"Philip suffered with bronchial asthma for a long time," Gloria sighs. "Then God answered our prayers and he outgrew it when he was about eight years old. When we went home on furlough the second time, the doctors tested him for allergies. He was allergic to common household dust! No wonder he was suffering! During dry season, it is a dust bowl in Bangladesh."

Gloria remembers sitting on the ferry with Philip. "He'd wipe and blow his nose endlessly, but he never complained. He never asked why we wouldn't leave this place that was making him sick. He accepted the fact that this was our country, and the Lord honored his commitment and took that illness away!"

Before David was a year old, the Thurmans were sitting in their living room one night in Faridpur. Don and Helen Jones, missionary neighbors, were there; Helen was holding David and noticed that he had some fever.

As she handed David to Gloria, he began convulsing in her arms. "I remember how helpless I felt as I sat there and held him. He had such hard convulsions. I knew the nearest doctor who would know anything about convulsions was six hours away in Dhaka. So we did all we knew to do. I held him to keep him from hitting his head or hurting himself in any way. Finally, the convulsions subsided and we started making plans to go into Dhaka the next morning."

The doctors in Dhaka checked David but found nothing alarming except a sore throat, but until he went to boarding school in the sixth grade, he continued to have febrile convulsions.

On their next furlough, Tom and Gloria consulted doctors in the States; they couldn't say whether the fever triggered the convulsion or the convulsion triggered the fever, but almost every time David had a convulsion, his throat was involved. The doctors thought the convulsions were fever related. They prescribed phenobarbital.

Grateful for medical advice and eager to care for her son appropriately, Gloria administered the prescribed dosage. Soon she began to notice a change in his personality. David had always been a happy child, but he became cross and ill while taking this medication. Gloria could find nothing to please him.

When the Thurmans returned to East Pakistan after furlough, they went to see a Presbyterian missionary doctor, Ted Kuhn. Gloria had a record of when David's convulsions took place and the severity of each. She could see that the intensity and regularity had lessened. Dr. Kuhn told her that was a good sign and he would probably outgrow them completely. He also said, "I would quit giving him the phenobarbital and risk a convulsion or two a year as compared to what the side effects of this strong medicine could do to him."

That was all the Thurmans needed to hear, because that was exactly what they felt, also. With heart-wrenching faith, the Thurmans did away with the medicine. "We knew many people were praying and we depended on those prayers," Gloria said. "We began to see a difference, but the convulsions didn't stop. They continued, even at boarding school. That was the main reason David's going to boarding school was so hard on Tom and me. We imagined him falling somewhere during a convulsion. We wondered who would take care of him after a convulsion, because they sapped him completely for as long as ten hours."

They knew that he needed to go to boarding school. David needed a better learning environment; he needed the discipline of study. Gloria had taught him at home, and she felt that he was not ready for boarding school scholastically, but emotionally, he needed to get away from his over-protective parents. Off to boarding school he went, to India in the foothills of the Himalayas. Philip was already in school there at Woodstock in Mussoorie, India.

"The most difficult time with the convulsions was that first year at Woodstock," Gloria recalls. "We went to see the boys and one night while we were there, David had three convulsions. It was a frigid night. Mussoorie was so cold; ice was everywhere. The little house where we were staying had no heat except for a little kerosene stove. There was a fireplace and we bought some firewood to make things a little warmer. We had discovered a long time ago that the Bengali way to handle a convulsion was to pour cold water on the patient's head. This always helped David. So we sat on the edge of the tin bathtub, held David, poured cold water on his head, and tried to keep him bundled up at the same time. He just went from one convulsion to the next. He had never done that before."

For the next two days, David was limp. He didn't talk; he didn't eat. Then on the day Tom and Gloria were to leave, he was able to go to church with them.

"David was standing by me," Gloria tells, "and I saw his knees begin to buckle. I told him to sit down quickly. We sat together and he jerked a couple of times. However, by the time the choir finished singing and we had the closing prayer, he was able to stand up and go to lunch. He was fine. We felt God was giving us assurance that it was going to be all right. As far as we know, and David knows, that was his last convulsion. God made it all right."

The Quack Clinic

Perhaps her sons' illnesses made Gloria sensitive to other sick children in and around Faridpur. In a letter home in 1970, Tom wrote for the first time about Gloria's clinic.

"Gloria is busy with an informal, non-professional clinic each afternoon for one hour. She wipes sores, gives aspirin, and counsels with the heavyhearted. Many are healed and helped because we are here. Some have been under doctor's care but her soap, medicine, prayer, and love are used by Him. That 'cup of cold water' is a blessing in a land of weary souls in search of a better life."

Even before the Thurmans arrived in East Pakistan, Southern Baptist medical personnel were in the country. The Mission was hoping to receive permission from the Pakistani government to open a hospital. There was such great need, but permission was never given. For five years the Mission spent much time and money dealing with government officials, following directions to register doctors and nurses, filling out papers, dealing with minute details and restrictions. It was to no avail. East Pakistan had highly skilled medical missionaries whose hands were tied. Eventually, they all went to other countries where they could practice.

But there was so much need.

It was difficult for Gloria, untrained, to take any responsibility. "I treated only as I would treat my own boys, and no more," Gloria points out. "When anybody in the Mission came to visit us, I'd close the clinic immediately. I feared what they would say, especially the medical personnel. They never asked me not to do the clinic, to close it, but I worried."

It started with a half-dozen women coming with small children with high fevers, bloated stomachs, and the like. Gloria knew what she'd do for Philip and David. She said to Tom, "I just don't feel right not doing anything knowing there is nothing close by for these poor people. Do you think it would be all right to use some of our funds to do some first-aid treatment if I try to keep it on that level?"

They decided that she should use her limited knowledge to help the women and children. The "quack" clinic was born. And it grew and grew. The people would hear about a child with stomach disease who had been helped, or one with worm infestation or head lice or scabies. Scabies and burns became her specialty. She had simple remedies that were unheard of in East Pakistan: for scabies—soap and Ascaboil, for burns—Foil Ointment.

Burns were common occurrences in the Faridpur area. The cooking stoves are on the ground, a dug-out, mud-lined contraption. People were not careful with the fire. Children scuffled for food and were pushed into hot coals. They would come to the clinic and Gloria would treat them.

"It began with an hour a day, for several days a week," Gloria says. "Then we set two days a week; the numbers kept increasing.

"Shova, a Christian girl, became my helper," Gloria remembers. "She checked the people in. They would line up outside the gate and wait for two or more hours to see me. I limited it strictly to children and expectant mothers whom I helped with prenatal care. The crowds continued to grow. One afternoon I saw 173 children."

Gloria worked in her backyard. A storage house behind the missionary house was her clinic, primitive even by Bengali standards.

"I had a rule that I wouldn't see anybody until afternoon. Mornings were off limits because of the boys. I was responsible for their education. My family was so supportive. Many times supper was late because I was exhausted from clinic.

"Once David had a hard convulsion in the middle of clinic. I simply said to the women that my own child was sick and I needed to take care of him. They were understanding; they would come back the next afternoon. They took their sick children and went home."

Certainly the most spectacular piece of medical work accomplished in the "quack" clinic, was the birth of Samson. In the spring of 1971, East Pakistan was in turmoil; war seemed inevitable. The Pakistani military came to Faridpur. Most of the women had gone into hiding, but one woman, Nira Dey, whose time for delivery was very close, simply could not go. She went, instead, to the back porch steps at the Thurmans' house. Tom went out to speak to her and she said, "If the military comes, they will have to shoot me here on your steps. I can't run any farther. Please let me stay with you."

Tom and Gloria saw the distress of the poor woman, and they felt they had no choice. She had to stay. They took her to one of the boy's rooms, where she protested over the bed, and asked for a plain mat on the floor. She stretched out, as best she could, on the mat that afternoon.

Tom said, "Do you have an emergency medical manual, Gloria?" She nodded.

"I think you best read it, and read it quickly," he advised.

Carl and Jean Ryther were still on the Faridpur compound. Carl was an agricultural missionary who worked with animals. "Oh, there's nothing to it. Don't worry about it," he said as he took off on "cow" business.

Tom piped in, "I will take care of the boys and pray," and he left the scene. Birthing was not Tom's strongest area of service.

Gloria and Jean read the medical manual. They put scissors, razors, gauze, and strips of material in four canning jars. They put the whole lot in the pressure cooker and sterilized everything.

Before sundown, Nira began to call. As time drew near, Gloria and Jean read and re-read the book. The thing Gloria really dreaded was cutting the umbilical cord. What if she cut the wrong place!

Jean got a little stool and sat right at Nira's feet. Gloria sat on the mat where Nira lay, talking to her, consoling her.

Jean said, "I'll read the book and tell you what's happening."

However, as it came time to deliver, Gloria looked up at Jean and saw that she was wet with perspiration. "Are you going to faint on me?" cried Gloria.

Jean mumbled, "I think I'd better go out for a little air." She put the book down on the stool and out she went!

The baby arrived without further complications; Jean returned and read to Gloria as she tied the knot and cut the cord. They cleaned the baby; they did everything the book said to do, but when Nira sat up, she began to hemorrhage.

"It nearly scared me to death," recalls Gloria. "But I had heard somewhere about packing, so we did that and prayed. God answered our prayers for the bleeding stopped."

Nira stayed with the Thurmans for three days and then left. The baby was a strong, healthy boy. Tom suggested the name Samson. Nira agreed and Samson has been going strong ever since.

Cal Guy, professor of missions at Southwestern Baptist Theological Seminary, came to Bangladesh after the war. He went with Tom to the villages to observe what was being done. They came back in the afternoon during clinic. Gloria was giving out medicine and Dr. Guy was very impressed. "This is the finest bit of medical work I've seen anywhere," he exclaimed.

After Dr. Guy returned to the States, Gloria received a check for $500 from the Foreign Mission Board earmarked for the medical work of Gloria Thurman. For three years, periodically a check arrived. The Mission never argued about it. In fact, they were very supportive. Gloria was careful to use the money to buy medicine. She turned in receipts for every penny.

"It seemed to me that the attitude of the Mission changed about the clinic," Gloria maintains. "My attitude changed because everybody knew about it. The Foreign Mission Board knew about it."

Jim McKinley always teased his wife, Betty, and Gloria about being consulting doctors. They called each other to check out treatments and medicines. The McKinleys are now retired, so Gloria consults with James Young in Dhaka.

"I still treat a lot of burns," admits Gloria. "The local doctors know about this. In fact, I've had doctors send patients they have treated asking me to take over treatment."

Gloria has trained her household helper, Didi, to clean, apply medicine, and wrap wounds. As long as Gloria remains in Bangladesh, the "quack" clinic is open for business.

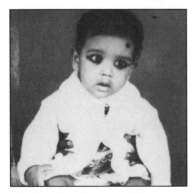

Gloria's first "birthing," Samson

The Lady with the Spot

"The most terrible sight I saw when we first came into Dhaka in 1965 were the beggars with leprosy," shudders Gloria. "A man suddenly appeared behind me, and I caught my breath in fright. He didn't have a nose, just a cavity, and you could see his teeth. One woman held up two stubs of hands, no fingers, no real hands. These extremes were all I had ever seen of leprosy. I knew East Pakistan was a land of lepers, 3 million of them, but it never occurred to me that I would be one of them."

Gloria went for her six-weeks post-natal checkup in November 1969. Recorded on her medical history was a notation that the patient had a ringworm on her left ankle.

"It was a little red circle, and the area around it stung like a bed of ants when I rubbed it on a sheet or anything," Gloria remembers.

The doctor gave her a salve for ringworm. She used one tube of the ointment and started on another. It didn't help at all. She asked for everyone's home remedy for ringworm; nothing seemed to help.

Months passed. One day in May, while Tom was away in one of the villages, Gloria was making up the bed. She hit the metal bed frame hard enough to make a dent in her leg—right where the circle was. There was no pain, no ache of any kind. She thought it strange that such a hard blow didn't cause any discomfort.

When Tom came in, she said, "I'll close my eyes. Take this pin and prick inside the circle."

Tom examined the site, poking and prodding. "I can't believe how deep I am sticking you," he commented. Gloria felt nothing.

The Thurmans were going to Dhaka in two weeks, so they decided to see a British dermatologist. When the doctor looked at the spot, he decided to take several scrapings from the ringworm circle." It didn't bother Gloria at all. Then he took clippings off both ears, a scraping from the top of her nose, both elbows and both knees. "Those scrapings all hurt a lot!" Gloria maintains.

Every place he took a nick with the razor blade, he covered with a Band-aid. "I looked like I had been in a battle," laughs Gloria. "I even had Band-aid earrings!"

Then he said, "Come back tomorrow for the report."

As they drove from the doctor's office to the Guest House, Tom asked, "What are you going to say tomorrow when he says leprosy?"

Gloria shot back, "It's not leprosy!"

Back at the Guest House, they read everything in the Foreign Mission Board manual about leprosy. There wasn't much to read. However, the manual did say that as far as they knew, no Southern Baptist missionary had ever had leprosy.

Gloria said to Tom, "Well we can forget leprosy. I don't intend to change medical history."

That night, they told the Mission family. None of them commented except to say that they were praying for Gloria. The next morning when they faced the doctor, Dr. Bassett asked, "Gloria, what do you think it is?"

"My husband thinks it's leprosy," she blurted.

"That's exactly what it is," he agreed.

Silence. Then Gloria demanded, "You have to tell us what to do. We are at the Guest House and there are many small children. We have a doctor and several nurses there as well. They may not want us to come back. Can I give it to them, to my family?"

"No, you have tuberculoid leprosy," he explained. "And you can be thankful for the ringworm, because the leprosy is enclosed inside the ringworm circle. There's no problem about going to the Guest House. No one can get this kind of leprosy from you."

Back to the Guest House they went to explain what they had learned about Gloria's leprosy. They offered to leave if anybody wanted them to do so, but everyone was supportive.

Two fellow missionaries, Troy Bennett and Trueman Moore, had to run an errand at a downtown hotel. Coming out of the hotel, they met a man who was leaving. They introduced themselves. He was with the World Health Organization of the United Nations, their expert on leprosy! He was in East Pakistan on a research trip.

"One of our missionaries has just been diagnosed with leprosy," Troy told him. "We have so many questions. You could help us."

Troy and Trueman brought him back to the Guest House for a question and answer session. Dr. Jeanne Beckett, who was waiting for the hospital that never came to be, knew all the right questions to ask. After the time together, everybody felt much better.

The Thurmans sent a report to the Foreign Mission Board. Baker James Cauthen, the executive secretary, was concerned. He told the Thurmans that the best medical care that could be found was available to them. Franklin Fowler, the medical consultant of the Board, sent word that they could use any facilities in the world.

Gloria jokingly remarked to the Mission family that they might accept her leprosy and the people in Faridpur might, but she didn't know about her family. Her own mother might not pick her up at the airport in Montgomery, Alabama!

Tom and Gloria knew they were in a country where leprosy was being treated daily. Dr. Bassett suggested they consider going to Chandragona to a Mission hospital run by the British Baptist Missionary Society which specialized in leprosy. "They have fine doctors and an excellent lab," explained the doctor.

They decided to go to Chandragona. The hospital made the extensive tests that the Foreign Mission Board required and sent their findings to laboratories in London. The Foreign Mission Board was not satisfied. They wanted biopsies sent to Carville, the leprosy treatment center in Louisiana. More biopsies were performed.

Almost verbatim the report came back from Carville to match the London reports. Tom and Gloria had peace of mind. Friends in the States were not so peaceful. Some sent sympathy cards and letters; some thought Gloria was in bed with her leg about to drop off. Some wrote Tom saying they wished they could come and cook him a good meal. Gloria tartly replies, "Tom was out in the village working. They would have to run him down to feed him!"

The newest medicine available, Dapsone, was purchased in Dhaka. The doctors suggested that Tom and the boys take Dapsone at its lowest level for one year as a precaution. When the Thurmans came home on their next furlough in 1973, Gloria went, at the Foreign Mission Board's insistence, to Carville for five days of extensive testing. Their report was the same as the one in Chandragona.

Gloria took Dapsone for three more years. On furlough in 1978, she was checked again in Carville. The doctor said, "Unless you ever have some symptom come up that causes you to question, you don't ever have to come back to Carville. Your record is clear."

She wondered how she might have contracted leprosy. The doctor explained that ordinarily a person gets leprosy through constant exposure over a long period of time. He said it could have happened in Alabama, one of the places in the US where leprosy is found.

They checked Tom at Carville, too. To Gloria's amusement they found a hard spot on his foot. She said, "Oh, I hope you have it so I can say I got it from you!" It turned out to be a simple corn!

"It was all right," Gloria says. "The leprosy was not too hard for God. I've had no trouble, no discomfort, and no sympathy! When I told my best friend in Faridpur, she looked at the little spot on my ankle and scoffed, 'You call that leprosy!' "

Tom wrote home in November of 1970:

It appeared for awhile that we might have to return to the States for treatment. We were willing to go if this were necessary, but we had come to feel at home here. We were meeting a real need; there had been response to our witness. Ten years ago, we had made a decision to come. This year we had to make the same decision in reverse—that is, to go. We carried this indecision for three months, and one night about midnight, we took our heavy load to Him. We prayed that if treatment necessitated, we would go home. It was then that He took our burden and gave us His precious peace. Then it did not matter if we went or stayed; we were ready to do His will.

During this experience, we came again to the truth of Dr. Cauthen's challenge at the time of our appointment in June 1964:

> I will sing unto the Lord,
> because He hath dealt
> bountifully with me.
> Psalm 13:6

We sing our best when we sing from the heart. Our wings of faith are stretched to soar into the darkness of the unknown. But, His Everlasting Arms are present to hold us up.

Gone with the Wave

November 13, 1970—the long, dark night of suffering, already called the worst natural disaster of the twentieth century. A half-million Bengalis were dead. Huge waves, swept by typhoon winds, brought death and destruction to a degree previously unknown.

Catastrophe is not a stranger to the land. Trygve Bolstad and Eirika Jansen in their book, *Sailing Against the Wind*, document that Bangladesh has about 15,000 miles of rivers, streams, and canals in a country about the size of Arkansas. Three major river systems, the Ganges, the Brahmaputra, and the Meghna, form the world's largest delta, twice the size of the Mississippi delta.

"The presence of these three large rivers, the heavy monsoon rainfall, and the low-lying nature of much of the country make floods an annual and inevitable phenomenon."

The authors add, "The extent of flooding depends upon the severity of monsoon rains. Moderate floods occur on the average once every 4 years, severe floods every 7 years and catastrophic floods once every 30 to 50 years. Both in 1987 and 1988, Bangladesh experienced catastrophic floods."

The tragedy of November 13, 1970, was beyond catastrophic.

In his book *Death to Life: Bangladesh*, Jim McKinley writes, "Just before midnight on November 13, a killing wave of water swept across the coastal area of Bangladesh, one of the most densely populated and least developed areas of the world. Some claim that in the immediate coastal area the wave was 30-feet high."

The tide was coming in about the same time the storm struck land. It was a cyclonic storm. Nobody knows how many miles inland the wall of water went. In some places people saw evidence 20 miles from the coast.

The water came in with fierce force. Then with a great surge, it rushed back to sea. Everything in its path was swept into the sea.

Jim McKinley and his family were living in Feni which was the closest Baptist Mission station to the coastal area. There was some road access. However, Jim had to walk many miles to get in the area hardest hit. There were no developed roads to the sea coast where most of the devastation occurred.

Jim describes the first trip he made into the area along with fellow missionary R T Buckley: "In one area the water came up a river channel. Then it gushed across the level rice fields without giving any attention to hundreds of little houses. An earthen dam caught this water and tried to turn it back toward the river. This only made the water swirl, tearing apart the little houses that had not already been ripped to pieces."

Rice straw was heaped several feet deep everywhere. For days men dug through the mountains of straw, finding the bodies of oxen, goats, chickens, and human beings.

As the two men followed the vicious path of the water, they saw that tons of earth had been pushed aside by the waves. When they reached the coast, after walking hours and hours through unimaginable destruction, a Bengali man said, "Come let us show you everything. Just come and walk with us."

"The stench of death was everywhere," explains Jim. "We walked around the bodies on the earthen dam near the ocean. As the water had rushed in, it had destroyed parts of the dam. But destroying it was not necessary here. The wave was high enough to pour over the top to kill and devastate. Little villages inside the dam had been as brutally beaten as those outside. This had been a killer."

In most of the villages in the immediate coastal area, few people if any had survived. One young man had open bleeding wounds on his chest. He had climbed a palm tree, covered with stickers that had torn into his chest as he clung on for his life. Jim asked him how he endured the pain and he answered, "I did not know there was any pain. I only wanted to live."

Tom Thurman said, "The cry of an old woman whose family had been swept away; the wail of an old man who lost everything he had was heartbreaking. We had to do something to help."

The Mission made the offer to do whatever the local government officer suggested. "Could you put down tube wells?" he asked.

The immediate need was for pure drinking water.

The procedure was simple: A small hole was dug. A simple wooden frame was placed over the hole. The workman then placed a long one-and-one-half-inch diameter galvanized pipe into the hole. A lever was attached to the pipe and to the wooden frame. One man climbed the frame and poured the pipe full of water. The water overflowed and filled the hole to cut off all air.

One man remained on the frame and placed the palm of his hand over the open end of the pipe. Another man pushed down on the lever lifting the pipe. He quickly released the lever, letting the pipe hit the bottom of the hole. Just as it hit, the man on top lifted his hand momentarily, letting the muddy earth squirt up through the pipe. The process was repeated rapidly. Down about 25 feet was safe drinking water. After the well was sunk, they pulled out the pipe. A filter was fastened to the end of the pipe. The pipe was put down again, and a little hand pump was fastened to the pipe.

Jim said, "We prayed as the pump was primed. The Muslims called out to Allah. Would the water be fresh or salty? No one knew until it had been tasted."

Rarely did they find fresh water on the first try. If they didn't, they'd move to another place and try again. When they did reach fresh water, the word went out. From every direction people came with all sorts of containers for "precious water."

The Mission sank tube wells in 200 villages. Jim and R T were joined by missionaries Don Jones, Carl Ryther, and Tom Thurman. They walked many miles carrying pipes and pumps to remote areas where no vehicle could go. They ate (and sometimes fasted) and slept in the villages. They worked long hours with the smell of death in their nostrils.

The need was so desperate; they worked man-killing hours under the broiling sun. Each day began at 3:30 A.M. At every site they encountered parents wailing for lost children.

Jim tells of one experience with a grieving mother: "I heard the pitiful cry of a woman. I had been moving quickly to make sure the work was proceeding as fast as possible. This, of course, was not the first time I had heard women wailing in the area, but I felt compelled to stop. I saw her on the little path.

"Her voice shrieked as she screamed out to Allah, 'I want my baby! I want my baby!' Pain rang out from this troubled soul. Dozens of other mothers in villages nearby were crying out only for this mother but also for hundreds and even thousands who had lost their little ones.

"I tried to think of some of the ways it had happened. Some had climbed trees with babies in their arms. The physical strain was too much. The babies slipped and then fell down into the devouring water. Most of the babies were never seen again. Others, frightened when the wave thundered into the village area, had their babies plucked from their arms as they stood helplessly in the swirling water. But perhaps even more tragic were the mothers who, when they heard the roar of the wave and then felt the water strike their feet, could not remember where their little ones were lying."

The toll, the fearful numbers who died, was not the whole story. Those left behind were emotionally drained and crippled.

"The tragedy of the tidal wave in 1970 shocked us as a Mission," Tom states. "It drove us to do something. That which we could do, we must do. From that day, we have been much involved in trying to meet human needs. We became identified as people who care. May it always be so."

Gloria's morning wash at the tube well.

Even the Skies are Weeping for Bengal

The Muslims in Hindu India had pushed for a state of their own for at least four decades. Jinnah, the Muslim League leader who became the first president of Pakistan, declared that one day there would be a Muslim state on the Indian subcontinent.

He was right. In 1947, independence came. India gave up two areas, West Pakistan and East Pakistan. The two sections were separated by a thousand miles. It was said that during those days the only two things that kept the two sections together were Islam and the Pakistan International Airways.

West Pakistan was the seat of power. Heavily populated East Pakistan was constantly agitating. The West wanted the state language to be Urdu. The Bengali-speaking East Pakistanis were determined to keep their language. Confrontation came in 1951 as riots broke out at Dhaka University; students were demanding that the language be Bengali. Three young men were killed by the police. The blood of these three became the seed bed out of which independence was finally to come.

Through the 1950s and 1960s, East Pakistan lived under martial law. An election would be called; elected officials would serve perhaps three months, and martial law would be imposed again.

By 1968, when the Thurmans had been in the country about three years, they realized that something was going to happen.

"I never envisioned that East Pakistan would break away from West Pakistan," vows Tom Thurman.

The military leaders in the West called for a free election. In East Pakistan there were, at that time, 72 political parties. The West thought there would be no unity in the East. No one would be elected to the National Assembly.

Something happened. Most of the political parties in East Pakistan joined together to support one candidate: Sheikh Mujibur Rahman of the Awami League. When the vote was counted, Sheikh Mujibur Rahman won the election.

It became clear almost immediately that West Pakistan would not accept the rule of an East Pakistani. Negotiations for the transfer of power took place, but nothing was resolved. Back and forth the delegates traveled. West Pakistan simply would not surrender the controls of the government.

On March 7, 1971, Sheikh Mujibur Rahman called a meeting in Dhaka. He was convinced, after fruitless negotiations, that the reins of power would never come to East Pakistan. He called for the independence of East Pakistan. There were massive demonstrations; all public officials went on strike. The post office was closed. Rail lines and boats ceased to operate. East Pakistan was paralyzed.

Although negotiations continued, West Pakistan used the time to bring in thousands of troops from the West. When they felt strong enough, they struck. On the night of March 25, 1971, the West Pakistan army sought to bring an end to the resistance. Fires were set all over Dhaka; the army began shooting and looting.

The streets of Dhaka were filled with tanks, trucks, and troops. There was heavy fighting which spread to Chittagong; eventually the whole country was at war.

In Faridpur, the Thurmans received a telegram from the American consulate urging them to go to Dhaka for possible evacuation.

"We had been listening to the news trying to hear what was going on. We heard that Dhaka was under siege," remembers Gloria.

"We knew the tanks had rolled out against the common man. We were anxious for our fellow missionaries in Dhaka as well."

Tom takes up the story, "We knew the ferries were probably closed down, and the busses had stopped. There was nothing heroic about our staying in Faridpur. We just decided to stay put where we were known. Philip and David were small—five and two. It would have been a hard trip for them."

In about a week, Carl and Jean Ryther came from Dhaka with their son, Tim. Carl's classic statement was, "We left Dhaka to come home to Faridpur because the military won't come to Faridpur."

Gloria chuckles, "We often reminded him of that statement in later days. One thing was for sure, Carl Ryther is no prophet!"

The Faridpur Mission House is located directly opposite the police lines. There was a large entrenchment of Bangladesh guerrillas, the freedom fighters.

"We knew that would be the battle line and we suspected the Baptist Mission could be a battle ground as well," says Tom.

On April 21, the military arrived. Gloria remembers, "We could hear as early as 4:30 A.M., the first sounds of the cannon. The night before, people were running in front of our house all night crying that the military was coming. We knew the boats had landed because we heard the shelling of the guns. All day they came closer and closer. That had to be the longest day we have ever lived!"

The school, the Christian Industrial Center, was still operating. West Pakistan had decreed that all things were to keep operating. Things were to remain normal. If anyone closed a business, they were suspected to be the opposition, but as the firing got closer, Tom and Carl decided the school should be closed. The Bengali wives and children had left to go to the villages already.

The army arrived in force in the afternoon, shelling the town. One shell hit the roof of the Christian Industrial Center, right in the compound. Although the facility was damaged, the people were safe. They had dismissed school and God had protected.

The Thurmans and the Rythers hit the floor in the Thurmans' house. Lying under the bed, David asked, "Dad, are you afraid?"

"He wanted to know if it was all right to be afraid," Tom sighs. "I told the boys that the military was not there to kill us. We are not in danger in that sense. We are only in danger as everybody else is.

"Night came and with it a stillness I had never before experienced," says Tom. "The sky glowed from all the burning buildings. Nothing moved except the military. We spent a sleepless night."

It was announced the next day that anyone harboring a Bengali would be punished severely. The Thurmans had a special visit by the military warning them of this rule, so they instructed all the Bengalis to go over the back fence if they saw the military coming.

Late in the afternoon of that day a group of 11 young men came from Dhaka to check on their families. When they reached Faridpur, they found it occupied. They came to the Thurman's house. Tom explained that they could not stay.

"We have no place else to go. Let us stay tonight and tomorrow we will find our families," they pled. So they stayed, and they stayed the next day as well. There was no way to leave without being seen by the military. None of them had ever done yard work before, but that day they put on *lungis* and worked.

Gloria explains, "We had a long row of hibiscus in front of the house. They dug them up, divided them, and transplanted them all around the house. Our house was a showplace for years to come!"

That night the young men slipped over the back fence, one by one, and escaped into the villages.

"If the military had come to our house the night before," Gloria states, "the young men would have been killed and we would have been, too. The Lord protected us all."

The military went to the demonstration farm that Carl Ryther managed and killed all the cows and chickens and ate them. Carl had two cows on the compound, and he decided that they should eat them before the military demanded them. There was no refrigeration, no electricity, so they shared the beef with the Christians and many Muslims. They ate all they could hold. Then Gloria and Jean started grinding to make salami. Jean made casings out of cheese cloth and Gloria seasoned, mixed, and stuffed the casings. They smoked the salami for four days. Both women declared they never, ever want another bite of salami as long as they live, but later on, salami was the only meat some hungry missionaries had.

Two memories of those besieged days in Faridpur remain more vivid than the others. The military burned the town when they arrived. Afterward, Tom went to the smoldering remains of the little shops. During the two years that the Thurmans had lived in Faridpur, Tom walked by the shops several times each week. He always greeted the shopkeepers, raising his hand in the Muslim greeting. They never acknowledged him, but that morning they grabbed his hand and expressed their appreciation for his coming. They said, "We have courage because you are still with us."

The other indelible memory has to do with the monsoon rains. It rains very little in April. In 1970, 3 inches of rain fell in April, but in 1971, they had 23 inches. A Bengali man, Mr. Munshi made a statement that touched the hearts of the whole world. Tom shared it with *Time* news correspondent, Dan Coggin, who used it as his lead: "Even the skies are weeping for Bengal."

Destination Dhaka

The first of the perilous month of April 1971, the McKinleys were in Feni and the Thurmans were still in Faridpur. Transportation was highly uncertain. Bridges had been destroyed; the roads were mined. Telephones were out or sporadic at best. Both families were uncertain of the whereabouts of the other. Listening to the Voice of America, they heard that an American evacuation had taken place from Dhaka. Uncertainty prevailed.

Then one afternoon about five, Dhijen Baroi arrived at the Faridpur compound with a letter from Jim McKinley. He had come by rickshaw and baby taxi, and had swum two rivers. It had taken him two days to make the journey. In addition, Dhijen was a young man and any young man might be suspected of being a freedom fighter and could be shot on sight by the military.

Jim's letter said, "We are still in Feni and wonder if you are still in Faridpur? We plan, when things settle down a little bit, to proceed to Dhaka. If you are in Faridpur, when you get a chance, go to Dhaka. Let's try to stay in touch."

Tom said to Dhijen, "You have already done a wonderful thing for us. Now we know the McKinleys are still in Feni. Would it be possible for you to return with a letter for the McKinleys?"

Dhijen answered immediately, "I can go. Let me visit with my family here in Faridpur and tomorrow morning, I will go."

Tom prepared a letter for Jim and Dhijen took it to him. He was a man of great courage.

On May 5, the Thurmans left for Dhaka. Gloria packed one suitcase with things they counted important and one change of clothes for each of them. As they left the Mission house, Tom turned to Gloria: "Remember Lot's wife. Don't look back."

The little band of pilgrims started to Dhaka. They traveled for nine hours by boat. Exhausted, they finally reached the dock at Aricha, on the Dhaka side of the ferry. A coolie came asking to help. They gave him the suitcase and he insisted on carrying David as well. He also helped them find a bus going to the city. When he deposited the suitcase and handed David to Gloria, Tom tried to pay him.

The coolie protested, "Oh, no, *Shaib*, this is a very hard time for you. I cannot take your money. You needed my help today, and I wanted to help you."

Tom shakes his head, "We knew these coolies. We knew this young man was trying to make his daily bread, but he refused our money because he saw the plight we were in."

As the Thurmans boarded the bus, they found it surrounded by the military. The soldiers were surprised to see a foreign family with small children. They began to talk excitedly among themselves, "Who are these people?" "Where are they going?"

One man came to their aid by saying, "I don't know who they are, but I do know they are Chinese."

The "Chinese" Thurmans made it to Dhaka and were reunited with the McKinleys, the only other Southern Baptist family left in war-torn East Pakistan.

After three weeks in Dhaka, the situation calmed. Tom and Gloria decided to make a quick trip to Faridpur. They wanted to let the people know that they were all right and that they were planning to stay in the country. The consulate advised Tom and Gloria to go, but they insisted that the boys remain with the McKinleys.

They made the trip to Faridpur with no problems. They packed another suitcase and loaded up some of the infamous salami. Food was scarce in Dhaka. On the trip back to the city, they planned to spend the night with some Christians in the town of Manikganj. However, as they reached the town, the military was there in force. The major requested that Tom and Gloria come to military camp.

Tom and Gloria declined the "invitation." "We're perfectly fine; here are our registration papers. We have friends in town. We'll spend the night with them." Under no conditions did the Thurmans want to be associated with the Pakistan military.

The soldiers refused to allow Tom and Gloria to go into town.

Tom protested, "We can't go on to Dhaka tonight. There are no ferries nor busses running. We'll just go on into town."

"You will come with us," they commanded.

They went with the military into their camp. They were taken upstairs to a little room.

"It was another long night," Gloria recalls. "I spread one sari across the bed since there was no bedding. Tom slept, but I could not. All night military boots went up and down the stairs. I didn't know if they were coming to our door or not."

"About 3:30 A.M. we discovered why they didn't want us to go into town. They burned the town that night. We could hear people screaming. We could hear shots being fired. We realized that people were being shot down like animals as they ran from the fire."

Even before daylight, Tom and Gloria left the camp. They didn't want a Bengali to see them coming from that place. As they passed the guards, Tom said, "We must leave now for Dhaka."

In spite of danger, Tom visited Faridpur throughout the summer to encourage the people. By August, however, things were getting hotter. The freedom fighters were making their presence known.

In October, Tom decided he had to make a trip to Gopalgonj. They had very little contact with the Christians in the two churches in the area: Gopalgonj and Orakandi.

It took a whole day to travel from Faridpur to Gopalgonj. Tom spent the night and started early the next morning for Orakandi. Going by boat, he had to pass three check points. The first was Pakistan military. They stopped the boat, and said, "Hands up!"

Tom put his hands up and they ordered him out of the boat. After they looked at his registration papers, they allowed him to go on.

A few miles down the river, he was stopped by freedom fighters. They said, "Hands up!" Up Tom's hands went again. As he stepped out of the boat, he was greeted by some of the young men. They had seen Tom going to Orakandi many times. Many had been educated at the missionary school in Orakandi. He was a friend. He got back in the boat and continued his journey.

The third stop was Pakistan military. They said, "Hands up." Finally, Tom reached Orakandi.

"That night I spent the night in Orakandi," Tom says. "The whole area had been heavily Hindu, and most of the people had fled to India. Christians were left along with a few Muslims. As I looked across the fields, I could see a lantern here and then, far-away, another one. There was an eerie silence. I realized that the people left in Orakandi were sheltering freedom fighters. If they were discovered, there would not be an Orakandi anymore. That didn't happen, for which I thank the Lord."

December arrived. Both families knew the war was escalating. They stayed close at the Guest House. They needed each other and depended on each other.

"The McKinleys are strong people," Tom declares. "We were the weaker ones leaning on them. Our children became so close. Philip fell while walking on the Guest House wall and broke his arm. Cherie and Kathy McKinley were so attentive to him and to David, too. They were little mothers to them. Keith and Wade McKinley were close in age to our boys and they were great friends."

The last opportunity to fly out of Dhaka came in early December. Both families prayed about leaving. But neither family left. In fact, only four-year-old Wade McKinley mentioned anything about it.

"Aunt Gloria," he drawled, "do you know why we didn't go?"

"Why, Wade?" Gloria asked.

"Because," he continued, "in America you can't buy *muri*."

Muri is the puffed rice that Bengalis eat for breakfast. Gloria laughs, "I know that *muri* was the primary topic of discussion for the McKinleys during the war!"

From December 4 until December 16, night bombings shook the city. The skies were ablaze. India entered the fight on the side of East Pakistan. India's planes dropped bombs as well as leaflets which read, "We are not after civilian targets. Stay clear of the Pakistan military. They are the ones we are after."

The beleaguered families bedded down in the hallway on the first floor of the Guest House. They put their mattresses on top of tables and slept underneath. During one of the really bad nights, Philip asked, "Daddy, if you'll hold my hand, I won't be afraid."

That night in their family prayertime, Tom prayed the same prayer: "Oh, Lord, if You will hold our hands, we won't be afraid."

To assure their families during the anxious days, Gloria wrote:

"In all that has happened, God has been very real. He has protected us from harm and given His peace in troubled days. He has taught a clearer meaning of bearing the burdens of one another. We believe that after great suffering God is able to do great things.

"The people continue to come and we continue to listen. If they find something of God's love, then our staying will not be in vain."

Joi Bangla!

"December 16, 1971, Bengali and Indian military forces had Dhaka surrounded," reported Jim McKinley in his book, *Death to Life: Bangladesh*. Everyone knew that close to 40,000 Pakistani soldiers were well fortified in the city. The commander of the Pakistan forces, General Niaza, had vowed to fight to the last man.

In the very center of the fortifications sat the Baptist Guest House with the McKinleys and the Thurmans. Next door, Troy, Marjorie Bennett and their daughter, Debbie, who had returned before the siege, were housed. Jim said, "We were sitting in a death trap."

Then flashed over the radio unbelievable words: "General Niaza has been ordered to surrender his forces in East Pakistan!"

December 16, 1971—*Joi Bangla!* Victory for the Bengalis! That handful of faithful missionaries witnessed the birth of a nation—the world's eighth largest in population. Bangladesh was born!

Hundreds of fully armed Pakistan soldiers moved north up the road by the Guest House, going to surrender. Within the same hour, the Bengali and Indian soldiers poured into the city, down the road by the Guest House.

"We were the welcoming committee," Jim claims. "We were caught up in the excitement of freedom. The children stood by the gate waving wildly to the victorious soldiers as they entered the city."

Gloria helped Cherie and Kathy make a Bangladesh flag which they raised to the top of the Guest House. Marj Bennett pulled out of hiding a little flag she had. The children waved that flag at the gate and were joyfully applauded. Victory had come! But along with the joy came an awesome responsibility.

Tom wrote: "We need an extra abundance of faith and love to help in the rebuilding. The task will not be easy. But we believe that God often asks us to take shattered pieces and begin to rebuild. I think this is the message of salvation, and we want to share it here."

Almost immediately after the war, Tom and Gloria had to deal with a test of faith concerning the Biharis. The Biharis are a group in Bangladesh who had come from Bihar in India. They spoke Urdu as did the people of West Pakistan. They always sided with their Urdu-speaking brothers. They were never assimilated into the population of East Pakistan. They were mechanics or held other technical jobs—very good jobs.

When the military took control of East Pakistan, they armed the Biharis. Tom says, "We heard awful tales of looting and raping. The Pakistan army was blamed, and they did a lot of it, but the Biharis did much, too. We knew when independence came, the Biharis would pay dearly. They were despised."

The Biharis were pushed to the back of the Thurmans' minds when the day of victory came. Tom and Gloria rejoiced with Bengali people and their thoughts turned to home—Faridpur. Oh, to be in Faridpur, in their own home, at Christmas!

Tom decided to make a trip to Faridpur to see if traveling would be possible. "Of course, I waited until later in the day to travel because there were still land mines in the road," he said. "I always let another vehicle go before me, which is always the charitable, Christian thing to do!"

Tom reached the river and crossed on a launch. "Nothing was moving except that launch," he recalls. "There was an eerie silence. When I got off the boat, I saw the reason. Three hundred or so corpses were floating in the water at Golando dock. They were Bihari soldiers who had been fleeing for their lives. They had been caught at the river and massacred."

Tom walked on toward Faridpur in a daze. After about five miles, he caught a ride in a military jeep.

"When I arrived in Faridpur," Tom says, "there was a great commotion on our compound. Right in front of the church, seven Biharis had been killed. The local people had caught them. Instead of shooting them, they had tortured them. When I got there, their blood was all over the church steps. The hate for the Biharis, the retaliation, was violent and terrible."

In Rajbari, the Bihari leader was stabbed, tied to a vehicle, and dragged through town. It was an awful way to die.

Tom shakes his head sadly, "The tragic thing is, we had this hatred toward the Biharis ourselves. We had seen what the Biharis had done to the Bengalis, and we felt hatred."

"I started praying," Tom says. "Lord, I'm a Christian and I can't have this hatred in my heart. Please help me to do something about these feelings toward the Biharis."

The business manager of the Christian Industrial Center, Mr. Mondal, came to the door and said, "There are three women here who want to see you."

All three were veiled with *burkas*, the traditional Muslim dress. They pulled back their veils and began telling their story.

"We are from Rajbari and we represent 700 women and children who are having a most difficult time. Our husbands were killed at Golando. We have come in desperation to the Baptist Mission to see if there is something you can do to help us."

"My mind clicked like the shutter of a camera," Tom declares. "I knew God was about to answer my prayer. I thought He'd do a miracle from heaven and take the hatred out of my heart. But He wanted me to remove that hatred."

"My ugly self wanted to say, 'You got what you deserved!' But my jaws just locked. I couldn't say a word."

After a long pause, Tom said, "Well, let me think and see what I can do." With help from the Salvation Army, Tom was able to help the distressed families. During that time of helping and serving, God removed the hatred from his heart.

The Bihari leader who had been so brutally killed in Rajbari had been married to a Christian, Chaya Qumar. When she married him, she was disowned and dismissed from the church. One day she, her aged mother, and her three children came to the Thurmans' door. Word had come that her husband's death was not enough. They wanted the blood of her two sons. The Thurmans had no choice but to take them in, although they knew the wrath of the community would be on their heads.

Several days later, a man came to see Tom. As he talked to Tom about Bangladesh, the man put a hand grenade on the table.

"I tried to ignore the hand grenade," Tom says shakily. "I told him how overjoyed we were at independence. I told him as Christians we were trying to help. I said that we loved everybody. Finally, he picked up the hand grenade and left."

Gloria takes up the story. "The community knew about our 'guests' and were very unhappy. We decided to move them to Dhaka where it would be easier for them to be lost in the crowd. Everybody knew there were two women and three children. We planned care fully. The mother, Chaya, would take one of the boys and the grandmother would take the other one. Tom and I would take our boys and the little girl. We went by bus, sitting separately, of course, with our designated children. The women wore their veils."

"When we boarded the ferry, I noticed two men talking about our boys and Esru, the little girl. It scared me to death. I eased over so I could hear what they were saying. They were amused to see one white-headed boy, one red-headed boy, and a black-headed girl."

"How can this be in one family?" one man asked.

The other said, "I'm not sure, but with foreigners, it happens!"

They made it safely to Dhaka. Gloria admits, "I went to Dhaka with a heavy heart. Three days after Chaya and her family came to us, some of the women on the compound saw one of them. Two of my dearest friends came to talk to me and told me why it was unwise for us to keep Chaya. They talked about how bad her husband had been. It seemed to me that their attitude was that she deserved the same fate. I tried not to be upset, but I was terribly hurt. Finally, I said that the Scripture said that he who was without sin, should cast the first stone. I asked them to think about that."

"If she had been your sister or your mother, would you have wanted me to take her in? They left and I did not see them before we left for Dhaka; they did not come back to our house at all. I had a real struggle, but I knew we had done the right thing."

"My friends came to see me when we got home from Dhaka. I told them that I had forgiven them for their attitude, but they needed to ask for forgiveness. They talked among themselves and then said, 'We were irrational; we realize that now. Please forgive us.' God took away the hurt and we remain good friends today."

"The sequel to Chaya's story is wonderful," Tom says. "Eventually, she was able to go back to Rajbari. She was accepted back in the church. She became head mistress of the school, a position she had held before the war. And those two precious boys, Stephen and Richard, are now very strong leaders in the church. We are happy for the little contribution we had in their lives."

Joi Bangla, but also, *Joi Jesus!*

Up from the Ashes

Independence came to Bangladesh, but the price was high. Villages and cities were smoldering ruins. Could this new nation survive? Could she rise up from the ashes?

Some 3 million Bengalis died in the bloody civil war. Ten million refugees were returning home from India, while an equal number of refugees were scattered about the country, living with relatives, in the jungle, in schoolhouses or other public buildings, and even in culverts. Few refugees found homes when they returned.

Jim McKinley says, "This was probably history's largest group of homeless refugees. Nothing symbolized the difficulty ahead more than that of a poor family gazing upon the barren earth where their little house, with all their earthly possessions, had previously stood. The scorched earth seemed to cry out in pain."

Many of the women bore scars more dreadful than the earth. About 200,000 had been raped by the Pakistan army. In the Muslim and Hindu cultures, they were no longer women, just "things."

Bangladesh was devastated. Four hundred and sixty-one bridges and culverts had been badly damaged or destroyed. Many ferries, the only way to cross the wide rivers, had been blown up or sunk. Rail lines were destroyed, and telephone lines were snapped.

Food supplies were dismally small. It seemed that all of Bangladesh was hungry. Word came of one village that survived on water hyacinths for over a month. War had kept the rice fields unplanted and untended; the fertile soil sprouted bushes and trees forming small jungles. Some rice paddies had been trampled while being used as a constant battle ground. Irrigation trenches had been ground to dust. There was no rice seed, no insecticide. How would 75 million hungry mouths be fed?

Cholera and smallpox had wiped out several areas. The wounds of war as well as the ravages of poor nutrition stalked the baby nation. Could the Land of the Bengalis overcome all this? Many doubted that it could.

But Thomas Thurman was not a "doubting" Thomas. He and Gloria, along with their boys, returned to Faridpur on Christmas Eve, just eight days after victory. Much needed to be done and they were eager to begin rebuilding. The people started coming to the Mission almost immediately for help.

"Within a 30-mile radius of our home there were 100,000 refugees," explains Tom. "Most of them had fled to India taking most of their property, whatever they could carry."

When they returned, their meager homes had been burned and looted. Anything of value—chickens, cattle, goats—was gone.

The new fragile government gave each family several large sheets of plastic and about $6 in money. They were to build a house with these paltry means. "But remember," Tom says, "that 10 million people were given the plastic and money—no easy feat."

June through September are miserable months in Bangladesh. The monsoon rains shower misery over the country. Villagers sleep on damp mud floors. After independence, many thousands were sleeping under the trees with only sheets of plastic over their heads."

As soon as the Foreign Mission Board made relief money available to them, Tom and Gloria began helping the people build simple houses. Each family was given 16 sheets of tin, each nine feet long. In addition, they were given *taka* 50, which is about $6.50. In all, the houses cost about $200 each. In the Faridpur district, 1,410 houses were built; 3,000 were constructed all over the country. They were inadequate by American standards, but to Bengalis exposed to monsoon rains, these simple houses were palaces.

Along with all the new problems, the old problem of hunger was ever present. In the land of the mighty rivers of the Ganges, floods continued to plague the people. Crops were destroyed. Cyclones blew, wiping out flimsy villages, but the rich earth tried to produce.

"Nearly 1,000 pounds of rice seed was distributed to the village people," Tom gladly tells. "I remember they ran their hands through the golden grain and left with smiling faces.

"They knew that in four months there would be rice. The lean days would not seem so long since there was hope for a little rice."

This rice did produce, but it was not a good crop. Tom maintains that he witnessed again the miracle recorded in the Bible of Jesus' Feeding of the 5,000. "From our seeds, 5,000 people were able to eat for five days. I was glad to be a part of God's miracle."

Out in the villages, the people were suffering. They were eating bark from the trees. They were cutting up grass to cook with onions to fill their stomachs. Undernourished children with swollen bellies looked to Tom and Gloria with big, sad eyes. Mothers reached out pleading hands; their children were starving.

"I cried out to the Lord for help," Tom says softly. "God sent help. The Salvation Army Medical and Social Team came from the Netherlands. They lived in our Mission house. They brought four nurses, an agriculturist, a mechanic, and a bookkeeper. UNICEF gave us high protein meal, which we took to several villages each day. Women stood in line for hours to get a cup of food. As they received their cup, children rushed to them as chicks go to a mother hen. The powdered food was on the faces of the children and we were glad that at least for one day that week, they had eaten."

During those dark days, the Baptist Mission worked with many groups in massive relief operations. Trucks would come into the compounds late at night. Around 3:30 in the morning, they loaded the trucks so that they could pull out at the crack of dawn. A man went ahead of them and gave out tickets. The tickets were presented and a can of high-protein biscuits were given in return. The Salvation Army provided the biscuits."

Many groups worked together to meet the overwhelming needs. What was needed most, however, was a good rice crop. The new year looked promising. Then a major flood occurred. The tragedy of 1974 was the worst ever experienced in the country. Starvation claimed 600,000. There was a major famine.

People from the villages went to Dhaka trying to find a piece of bread. It was estimated that 1,200 corpses a week were picked up off the streets of Dhaka. Some trucks picked up the dead, while other trucks picked up live bodies, some just barely. They were taken to a camp a few miles out of the city. Many did not live long. Graves were being dug constantly, but there were still many able-bodied men and women, and they were ready to work. Jim McKinley employed as many of them as possible in a food-for-work project.

The workers leveled land for a house building project; they dug ponds for bathing and for growing fish, and they built up roads so they could be traveled during the flood times. More than 3,000 of the world's most devastated people were working, getting stronger as they worked, and they were being paid well.

The Salvation Army team that came to Faridpur came prepared, bringing $500,000 worth of medicines and other supplies. Village clinics ministered to the people. Some of the people came 30 hours ahead of time to take their place in line. Tom says, "They slept on mats under the trees so that they might get their medicines. Hot fevered babies came, some with dysentery, running sores and ears. Sores covered the bodies of the children; men and women showed all of the diseases that go with neglect. We gave sulfa, aspirins, and worm medicines, and saw the people come alive. More came than we could help, but for nine months we were busy day and night."

Gloria is reminded of how thankful they were that they knew the language so that they could interpret for the groups that came.

After the war, the Foreign Mission Board sent a couple trained in social ministries, Louis and Barbara O'Conner, to Bangladesh. One of the most helpful and enduring tasks they accomplished was beginning a training center in simple carpentry for physically handicapped. Most of the trainees are crippled, former beggars learning how to make the simplest of straight chairs, stools, small tables, and benches. They make wooden crutches for crippled people. Tungi Rehabilitation Center helps beggars earn their living and helps crippled people walk. Hundreds of pairs of their crutches have been donated to the orthopedic hospital in Dhaka. Those who leave that hospital often walk on Tungi crutches.

Before the war, the Christian Industrial Center in Faridpur was busy training young men in technical trades. After two years of training a graduate could get a good job. Each year, 60 to 100 young men enroll each year.

Another facet of help was introduced at the Development Service Center. A 26-acre farm out from Dhaka, the Development Service Center has seven ponds for hatching and growing fish, three large goat barns, and a duck hatchery with the world's best layers. All of this is to help Bengalis learn how to feed themselves. They may buy any of the fish, goats, ducks, or eggs.

As tremendous human needs were being met, no missionary forgot that Bengalis needed not just bread, but the bread of life; they needed not only pure water, but Jesus, who gives living water; they needed not only physical healing, but the healing of sin-sick lives.

Tom Thurman said it best: "Bangladesh has been bound, bruised and chained. Now the chains are gone. A new day has come, and Southern Baptists are here to help set the people free."

The People that Walk in Great Darkness

A friend of the Thurmans said, "Bangladesh, and Faridpur in particular, has become very important to me. I know that God is ready and sufficient to pour out His magnificent and bountiful blessings on His people. I have grown to love these simple and beautiful folk. I respect them and marvel at their strength. They have been bent but have not broken. Like a jute stalk that is blown down, they will rise to grow again. Through all the misery and poverty, hunger, flood and wars, these people have managed to keep a smile on their faces, a song in their hearts, and a desire to build a better life."

This friend was correct. Through the fire and the flood, the Bengalis survived. Now the question: what could the Baptist Mission do to help the people and to reach them with the good news of Jesus Christ at the same time?

With the help of Donald MacGavern, church growth consultant from Fuller Theological Seminary in Pasadena, California, and Cal Guy, professor of missions at Southwestern Baptist Theological Seminary in Fort Worth, Texas, the missionaries developed a strategy for getting as many people as possible to respond to the gospel. A book was produced in simple Bengali outlining a chronological study of the life of Jesus: *The Man Who Gave His Life.* The English title is *The Man You Cannot Ignore.*

Previously, the Mission had Bible Book Rooms. The philosophy was that people who wanted to hear the gospel would go to these Reading Rooms to study and learn about Christianity. A lot of students, young men primarily, did become interested, but it was difficult for them to become Christians.

"Dr. Guy helped us to see that we shouldn't sit and wait for people to come to the Bible Book Rooms. We should take the good news out to the villages. So from that day onward, we have tried to let our work be village-centered," explains Tom.

After all, 94 percent of the people in the country are in the villages, where people walk in darkness, live in darkness.

The village concept was not difficult for the Mission to accept. However, Dr. Guy presented another concept that was hard for some to swallow. He said that in New Testament times, people responded to the gospel in a group. The Western idea is that every person makes an individual decision, but Bangladesh is part of the Eastern world where individuals function as part of a larger group.

"I wanted to believe this truth," Tom says. "I knew the Lord wanted to teach me, but I was slow to learn this concept."

Tom went to a village for a revival meeting. One of the men had an awful stomach problem which Tom suspected was an ulcer. The man couldn't sleep. He moaned and groaned so much that nobody else could sleep. Tom offered to take him to a good Filipino doctor in Gopalgonj whose specialty is stomach surgery.

The man thought awhile, then he talked to all his kinfolk in the village. He talked to his friends in the village. In a day or two, he sent runners to other villages to bring in other friends to help him decide. Finally, on the third day, they all agreed that the man should go with Tom to have the surgery.

"God was trying to teach me that the people in Bangladesh make decisions in a group," Tom points out. "In the West, I decide. In the East, the group decides. However, before anyone is baptized, each personally decides to accept Jesus. Sometimes even if the village decides to become Christian, some 'back-out' at the last moment. So the whole village doesn't become Christian."

"When we came to East Pakistan, all of us wanted to win all of East Pakistan to the Lord," Tom says. "I certainly did not understand that it would be by groups and some very different groups."

One such group was the Telegus. These people had been in Dhaka close to a century. They worked as street sweepers. The Telegus were there when Immanuel Baptist Church was beginning in 1963—outside, of course, sweeping the streets.

Some of them found the courage to enter the church and seek out the pastor. Simon Sicar, a most respected Bengali pastor, came with spotless credentials and a glorious ancestry. William Carey's first convert was the great-great-great grandfather of Simon Sicar. As pastor, Simon looked upon the Telegus with an open heart. He was joined in this venture by Jim McKinley who had stayed in Dhaka after the war. Together they shared the Lord with the Telegus.

One glorious Sunday, 54 Telegus were baptized in Immanuel Baptist Church. In those days, if Baptists had a dozen converts all over Bangladesh in all of the churches, they would have rejoiced— 54 in one Sunday was an electrifying experience!

"To see the well-to-do, well-dressed, well-educated members of Immanuel reaching out and loving new brothers and sisters who were sweepers," Gloria marvels, "was wonderful. Two different people, two different races, worshiping together in a beautiful way."

Before long, however, the Telegus wanted their own church.

They wanted to sing their own songs, they wanted to lead their own services, and they wanted to reach out to other Telegus. They not only started their own church in Dhaka, they also "mothered" another Telegu church in another part of the city. They remembered the tea-growing district of Sylhet where many Telegus harvested the tea leaves. They started a church there. Then their eyes turned to Ishurdi where many Telegus lived. In January 1985, a Telegu Church, Newsprint Baptist Church, opened its doors in Khulna, the second largest seaport in the country.

The Telegus were just part of God's miraculous moving in the country. When Southern Baptists first came to East Pakistan in 1957, it took six years before one church was begun. In 1963, Immanuel Baptist Church in Dhaka opened its doors. Slowly other churches were started, but after the new strategy was established, exciting things began to happen. At the end of 1992, many Baptist churches were reported.

"The thrilling thing," Tom says, "is that people in one village go to the next village to tell their kinfolks. The work is growing along family lines. How we pray that the 125 million people in Bangladesh in 68,816 villages will have a chance to hear the Word of the Lord."

In 1974 Tom and Gloria were asked to move to Dhaka for Tom to be the Mission treasurer. He told Dr. Hughey, then area director for Bangladesh, that if he was going to keep books full-time, he'd rather do it in Jackson, Mississippi. He did agree to train a Bengali staff and supervise them—from out on the field where God has called him to work. The decision has meant many trips into Dhaka to train and to check work, but God has blessed this decision, and Tom has stayed in village work.

Through the years, the Thurmans have asked Southern Baptists at home to pray with them for the lost villages of Bangladesh. One letter drew a poignant portrait.

Come go with me to the villages of Bangladesh to see the friendly
   faces of hundreds of children as they run along singing behind the
   motorcycle,
Smell the aroma of the freshly cut rice which is being trampled by
   oxen and winnowed for husking,
Touch the hand of an old man who reaches out in love,
Taste the delicious spices in the curry with hot rice,
Hear the vibrant voices of men, women, and children as they engage
   in the worship of Islam or Hinduism.
These are the villages for whom Christ gave His life, and a group of
   missionaries are in the land with the same mission.

The people walk in great darkness but today they are beginning to
see the light!

In the village of Hatbaria, walking in great darkness.

The Little Red School House

So what do you do when you live on the backside of nowhere and it's time for school? If you are Philip and David Thurman, you go to school in the little red school house at home. David says, "I got up from the breakfast table and said, 'Bye, Mom.' I brushed my teeth, came out and said, 'Good morning, teacher!'"

School normally began in mid-August. Gloria, was the teacher. She used the Calvert Correspondence Course which both boys began in kindergarten.

Philip spent first grade in Columbia, Mississippi, when the Thurmans came home on their second furlough. He knew more Bengali than English, and he renamed Gloria's mother "Bubba" because grandmother was too much to say. One day Philip called, "Mama, come to the kitchen. Bubba don't understand anything!" He had wanted something, but did not know the correct English word. Bubba did not understand *jinish*, the Bengali word for thing.

In 1974 the family returned to Bangladesh where *jinish* was a reg ular, ordinary word. Philip began second grade and David started kindergarten. Mornings were school times. Homework was to be done in the afternoons while Gloria worked in the clinic.

The boys were happy in school and Gloria enjoyed teaching them. They hurried to get school work done early so more interesting pursuits could be undertaken in the afternoons.

One of the more interesting pursuits was when the gardener taught the boys to swim. A big pond in front of the Thurmans' house was a perfect swimming hole. The gardener took Philip and David, tied a pair of ripe coconuts in the shell under their arms, then pushed the boys into the water. Gloria watched with much apprehension, yelling once in awhile for them to be careful.

Finally, the gardener said, "Madam, you go inside and do your work. If I need you, I'll call."

Chastened, Gloria went inside. After three days of "coconut floating," the boys could paddle. The coconuts were removed and they began swimming on their own.

The boys also used free afternoons to go into business. They set up a drink shop outside the garden wall. Three plywood sides of packing crates were tied to bamboo poles. Plastic sheeting made a good roof. A small table held eight plastic glasses. Lemonade and fruit drink went out by the jugs from Gloria's kitchen.

The boys enlisted Anima, a neighbor who doted on them, to make local snacks. She made popcorn balls with *muri*, the puffed rice, and date juice sugar. She also made the boy's favorite, *muri* fritters. Few fritters were sold before the profits were eaten!

The workers nearby enjoyed the cool drinks and snacks. Most of all, they enjoyed haggling over the price of the goods which was usually 25 *paisa*—five cents.

The packing crates of Alabama pine brought over in 1969 were used for much more than the drink stand. Kitchen shelves, tables in the house and schoolroom, were made from the hardy wood which is immune to Bengali bugs. However, the piece of crating that brought the most joy to the boys was the solid end of the packing box, a one-inch-thick board which fit perfectly in the branches of the big flame tree in the front yard. It provided a sturdy floor; with a small tent stretched above, it made an excellent tree house for Philip, David, and many of their friends. A metal step chair served as a ladder to enable the boys to reach the first limb for climbing.

Gloria and her two eager students have fun-filled as well as hectic memories of the bicentennial celebration of America's birthday. Philip, a fourth-grader, and David, a first-grader, enjoyed their history lessons about the founding of their native America.

As the grand finale of their studies, they planned a garden tea to celebrate. They invited the church members in Faridpur and approximately 50 other people for a morning tea following church services.

The boys prepared posters with pictures and explanations of the American flag, the national bird, the national anthem, the Liberty Bell, the Gettysburg Address, the 13 original colonies, the White House, and several other significant bits of history. They attached the posters to wooden stakes and displayed them in the yard throughout the garden area.

They even dressed for the occasion. Tom and the boys dressed alike in blue-and-white checked shirts, blue trousers, and red pocket handkerchiefs. Gloria wore a beautiful, long, blue-and-white checked dress with a red sash.

Refreshments consisted of cakes with red, white, and blue icing, party mix, mints, chicken salad sandwiches, and punch. Before the tea ended, two extra sheet cakes had been hurriedly put in the oven and were decorated with white glaze only. More than 400 people attended the big celebration!

Gloria laughs, "We were glad this happens once in 200 years!"

From 1976 through 1978, a journeyman teacher, Carol Hardin, lived on the second floor of the big Mission house in Faridpur and taught Oriana and Desi Kirkpatrick, children of Missionaries Tom and Beverly Kirkpatrick, as well as Philip and David.

After a furlough in 1978, the Thurmans returned to Bangladesh to face one of the most difficult challenges for missionary parents and their children—Philip went away to boarding school. A letter from Tom reflects their agony. "We leave tomorrow for Dhaka. Philip and I will depart Dhaka on July 20 for the journey to Woodstock School in Mussoorie, India. Even as we plan, we are like weeping willows, but we are claiming God's victory in this, too. We think he is ready for the seventh grade away from home. He is excited and we know this is the best thing for him."

Woodstock is in the foothills of the Himalayas. The trip began with a direct flight from Dhaka to Delhi, then continued with a bus or taxi ride for five or six hours up the steep, steep mountains. The school consists of students from several areas: one-third are missionaries' kids, one-third are foreigners, and one-third are Indian. It goes through grade 12 and is tough scholastically.

Philip was a good sportsman, so he managed to stay in the good graces of Woodstock authorities because he represented the school well. He played soccer and basketball. He broke the school record in high jump and pole vault.

Meanwhile, David continued to work with his mother until July 1981 when he, too, went to Woodstock.

"I felt David wasn't ready for boarding school," Gloria says. "But we decided it was best for him to break his ties with home."

After another furlough, both boys returned to Woodstock. Several months later, Philip wrote to his parents, "I think you need to know that David is not happy at boarding school. I talked to his counselor and he suggests that you come."

Gloria went to Woodstock. David's teachers confirmed what Philip had said. Gloria talked to David and they prayed together.

"David, it won't be easy for either of us if you study at home," acknowledged Gloria. "But, at the end of the term, bring all your things with you. We'll give it a try."

"It was as though a huge burden had been completely lifted," Gloria continues. "I couldn't believe the change that took place in his attitude. He had been miserable there."

David studied at home for the ninth and tenth grades. When he completed them, he decided to go to Harrison-Chilhowie Baptist Academy in Seymour, Tennessee, for one year. When Tom and Gloria came home for furlough five, David decided to graduate in Columbia, Mississippi, and live at home.

Philip had decided to go to Mississippi College in Clinton, Mississippi, his dad's alma mater. He loved Mississippi College and was excited when the school fielded a soccer team. In May 1989, Philip and fellow Bangladeshi missionaries' kid Tim Young were able to return to Bangladesh as members of the American Sea Horse team. They competed with the Bengali teams in National and Dhaka stadiums. They had arrived!

Philip met Lori Kinchen at MC. Tom and Gloria started getting a lot of letters saying, "Lori and I this. . . ." "Lori and I that. . . ." Then one day a letter came telling them what a good deal he had gotten on an engagement ring. He also revealed in that letter that he had gotten down on his knees and proposed after a soccer game.

"We are thankful God has sent a real treasure for Philip," says Gloria. "Lori's been willing to suffer with him as he seeks God's will for his life. We're thankful for her family's support and that they are a strong Christian family."

Philip and Lori were married in a beautiful ceremony August 4, 1990, in Jackson, Mississippi. Tom officiated, David was best man, and Gloria was the beautiful mother of the groom. Two years later, the young couple surrendered to full-time Christian service.

In September 1992, David also felt called to mission service. "What more could we ask?" say Tom and Gloria. "Both of our boys have surrendered to serve the Lord, and we know whatever they feel called to do or wherever they feel called to go, it will be all right!"

Fifty Miles Beyond the Great Commission

After ten years in Faridpur, Tom and Gloria had come to know the area south of them around Gopalgonj, a place referred to as "fifty miles beyond the Great Commission!" The Faridpur Baptist Church was a mother church of sorts, overseeing the church in Gopalgonj.

Once a month, someone would go to Gopalgonj to have children's camps or to work with the women. They would go on Friday and spend the weekend, making side trips to the surrounding villages, doing surveys. Tom kept thinking, "A missionary needs to be living in Gopalgonj."

Before leaving for furlough in 1978, Tom and Gloria expressed a desire to be sent to Gopalgonj when they returned.

While they were home in the States, the Mission voted for them to go to Rajbari which is to the north of Faridpur. The reasons to go to Rajbari were excellent: a good road existed from Faridpur to Rajbari, a better house was available, electricity was available.

There were compelling reasons not to go to Gopalgonj: no all-weather road from Faridpur, a five- or six-hour boat ride from Faridpur, no good housing, and little electricity.

The Thurmans, however, felt strongly that God was calling them to Gopalgonj. They expressed their feelings in no uncertain terms.

The selection of where a missionary lives is a three-way decision made by the Foreign Mission Board area director, the Mission, and the Bangladesh Baptist Fellowship. The Bangladesh Baptist Fellowship said, "If possible, go to Gopalgonj."

Finally, the others agreed for Tom and Gloria to go to Gopalgonj.

Tom rented a small, four-room house. He advanced some money for the landlord to put grills on the windows and the porch and to install glass in the windows, but the house was dark and very hot.

"We could lay in bed at night and right outside the window was the road," says Gloria. "We could hear what people in the rickshaws were saying as they passed within a few feet of us. You could actually touch people walking by. From the other window in the bedroom, you could reach in our neighbor's bedroom and pull the sheet off the bed. Too close!"

With a groan Gloria recalls the moving day to Gopalgonj. "The brother-in-law of the landlord loaded our household goods on a truck to take them to the boat and get everything down the river to our waiting house. His classic statement was, 'You all wait until ten o'clock in the morning and start your trip. I'll go early and we'll arrive about the same time.'"

The Thurmans boarded a country boat as instructed. Gloria insisted they take two suitcases with them. She had packed clothes for each of them for the night and the next day. As a precaution, she packed two bed sheets and four towels.

The six-hour trip put the family in Gopalgonj well before sundown, but there was no sign of their household goods. Gloria put a sheet in one bedroom for the boys and a sheet in the other for Tom and herself. They rolled up the four towels for pillows and bedded down for the first night in their new home.

The next day before lunch, word came that the goods had arrived at the dock, right down in the middle of town. The men had poled all day and all night. The coolies brought all the Thurmans' belongings on their heads. Gloria opened the bedroom door and they stepped from the street inside the house.

"We had a ten-foot refrigerator." Gloria chuckles. "It was funny to see three little men with the refrigerator turned sideways balanced on their heads! They bowed down to get it through the door. Of course, because of poor electricity, we could not use it."

Everybody in town knew everything the Thurmans owned. One man appeared at their door a week after the goods had arrived and said, "I want to see that pretty pink bedcover."

Gloria asked, "How did you know about the pink bedcover?"

"It was in one of the drawers of your *almira* (dresser)," the man answered. So Gloria showed him.

"I guess everybody opened and looked in the dresser drawers when they came by," Gloria surmised.

Their neighbors were fascinated that the landlord had been instructed to enclose the little building in the backyard. He was even asked to connect it to the house. After much persuasion and an advance on their rent, the landlord finally agreed to do it.

"Little did I know," Gloria declares, "that we had the show place for all of Gopalgonj! The first year we lived there, not a single day passed when we were at home, that someone did not come to see the bathroom attached to the house."

Gloria recalls that the bathroom was not really "up to snuff." The cement floor had been poured without the worker first putting down plastic. The result was a soppy wet floor all during rainy season. Tom called the man back and said, "My wife is upset. She is afraid someone will break a leg on the wet floor."

The man looked at the floor and thought awhile and then he pronounced, "Well, *Shaib*, you can put sand on it." The Thurmans decided that they'd take wet cement over sandy cement.

The kitchen in the tiny house would never get the *Good Housekeeping* seal of approval. The packing crate table held three kerosene burners. Tom and Gloria had an electric stove, but there was poor electricity. The refrigerator was useless as well. They had a hand pump outside and put a small water tank on top of the house. Water was pumped up early in the morning and again at night. They were very careful about how much water was used.

When they had visitors, it was a challenge. Dr. Bill Wakefield, their boss from the Foreign Mission Board, his wife Delcie, and Mrs. Rhoades, a Foreign Mission Board member came at one time.

"I put the women in the boy's room and Dr. Wakefield on a cot on the screened-in porch." Gloria sighs. "That night a driving rainstorm came up and it drenched him, but they were all good sports."

Tom's brother, Dennie, his wife, Joy, and their three children visited the Thurmans while they were in the little house in Gopalgonj. It was hot and they were miserable.

"I remember Joy sitting in the backyard with her daughter, J. J., fanning her. Philip was pumping water and pouring it on her feet which were sunk in a bucket. They decided a three-day visit was long enough. I can't understand it. There were only the four of us, a summer missionary, and the five of them in that hot little house!"

As Dennie and his family boarded the plane in Dhaka, he said to Tom, "I've sung 'Wherever He Leads I'll Go' all my life, with all my heart. But after being in Gopalgonj, I won't ever even hum it!"

Most of the inhabitants of Gopalgonj had never been around foreigners before, so the Thurmans were a source of wonder and amusement to them. They came day and night to look at Tom and Gloria and their unusual house.

"I will never go to someone's house to 'look,' not even the White House, after living in that fish bowl for four years!" Gloria declares.

"People would come and say, 'Can I just see this or that?' Our landlady felt real pride because it was her house. Anytime she had visitors she would bring them and personally show them everything. She even explained our clothes on the clothesline. She had never seen a pair of women's underpants. Nor had her visitor who asked, 'Who wears these?' The landlady said, 'Oh, they use them.'"

Tom breaks in, "It was hard living in this little house. While I was gone most of the time, Gloria bore the brunt of it. But she made very good friends in the Muslim community. People didn't know who we were at first. Some thought I was with the CIA. We started sinking tube wells and then they knew we were a helping agency."

In 1981, the Thurmans asked the Mission to buy property in Gopalgonj. They had decided to wait to see if people would be responsive in the area and they were. A house was to be built while they came home on furlough in 1983. They didn't ask for anything except plenty of windows for light and a breeze.

"The property was out in the country when we bought it," Tom explains. "But the town has moved out to us. The bus terminal is almost next door. The government has built offices and the police lines are just beyond us."

"It's a good house," Gloria adds. "It has 1,600 square feet and cost $32,000 (US money) in 1984 when it was built. It is light and airy. We have beautiful flowers in the yard and a good garden."

"Fifty miles beyond the Great Commission perhaps," Tom admits, "but God is blessing us. He sent Adhir and Shova Halder in 1981 to work in development. Adhir supervises putting down tube wells, gives out sanitary latrines, works with rebuilding houses, and works with the the tutorial and savings programs."

In 1983, He sent James and Dorothy Halder. And that begins a whole 'nother story.

And God Sent James and Dorothy

The Thurmans had been in Gopalgonj three years. Tom says, "I don't know how many miles we walked, how many villages we visited, how many people we met. Our work was agonizingly slow. Nothing was happening."

"Then God sent James and Dorothy Halder. All of a sudden, doors started opening. If we sound excited, it's because we are! If we sound thankful, it's because God has blessed us!"

James Halder is a native of Gopalgonj. Born about 15 miles from the city, he's a fourth generation Christian and the oldest son in a family of nine children. When he finished high school in 1967, he received a letter from Southern Baptist missionary Charles Beckett asking him to come visit in Feni. Charles Beckett offered James a job in the Reading Room at Feni.

James liked Feni. He liked the way the Baptists worked and preached. "I had no inclination, however, to work in missions," James says. "I really wanted to go into the Pakistani air force, but I was too young, so I decided to work in the Reading Room."

Only a month after he began his work, the Becketts went on vacation to Nepal for a month. They asked the Thurmans, who were in Comilla then, to supervise the new employee.

"So I met, for the first time, the Thurmans," James remembers. "Brother Tom asked me to come to Comilla to eat lunch with them. Being a poor young man, I accepted his invitation. That was the first time I met Sister Gloria and six-month-old Philip. I visited with them several times until they moved to Faridpur. After that, I saw them only at meetings."

Then the war came. James was working still in Feni with Jim McKinley. "The McKinleys and the Thurmans stayed during the war," James shakes his head. "I would say they loved our country very much to stay during those hard days. It was especially hard on foreigners. They could have gone home, but they knew we needed them. What they did, I can never forget."

After the war, James went back to Feni and the Thurmans returned to Faridpur. "I heard from the people in Gopalgonj that the Thurmans came to them," James says. "They had to go by motor launch. They began to love the area, the villages. It's very hard to go to the villages in the interior. You must go by small boat, but they never complained."

In 1974, the Baptist Mission changed its style of missions work to focus on village evangelism. James transferred to development work in agriculture and cattle. His supervisor was Missionary Carl Ryther, who headed that work.

That same year, a devastating flood hit the northern part of Bangladesh. UNICEF and the Baptist Mission were asked to help in the area around Jamalpur. Carl sent James to help.

"We helped destitute women and children in particular," James explains. "We operated 16 feeding centers, feeding 16,000. We had a food-for-work program, planting vegetables and wheat. I worked there for three years."

James tells of the plight of his own family and the fact that he felt much responsibility. "But I was not able to help them very much. I called to the Lord and He provided," James states. He found a wonderful job with UNICEF making a salary ten times more than he had been receiving.

Then James went to a Bangladesh Baptist Fellowship meeting where he learned that a scholarship for theological education was available, but that no one was interested in going to study.

"That shook me," James says simply. "I knew that I could tell my need to God, and He would hear. So I said to the Lord, 'Why not send me to go and serve You?'"

James asked several people to pray with him. He felt close to an Australian Baptist couple serving in Jamalpur, Dr. and Mrs. Ian M. Hawley. He asked the Hawleys to pray with him. He also asked Jim McKinley to pray.

Jim said, "You can go."

James answered, "There are many other good people who should go instead of me."

"Give me the names of those good people," Jim retorted.

James replied, "I understand what you are saying. But if I should leave my good job and my family, I want it to be God's call."

80

No peace came to James about the call, so he continued working for UNICEF. Two years later, he again heard a plea for someone to go to the seminary. He no longer resisted. He sent his application to the Bangladesh Baptist Fellowship and was accepted.

"They said I had to take my wife, and I had no wife," James says.

Tom Thurman said, "I have a good girl for you. Everything about her is good." But, James did not marry that girl.

Tom takes up the story: "We had a rule not to send a single man to the seminary, and I found another girl, Dorothy, for James. Dorothy's father knew James and liked him. He very much wanted his only daughter to marry a Christian preacher."

Dorothy was a city girl, born and raised in Khulna. Her parents were faithful church-goers. She had gone to a Baptist boarding school even though her background was Anglican. Dorothy did not want to marry a preacher. She had seen too many poor preachers with many children, lots of trouble, and too much poverty. But, her father arranged the wedding. James went to Khulna and met Dorothy, and three months later they were married.

In January 1979, the couple went to Baguio City to the Philippine Baptist Theological Seminary. There they both worked hard and studied hard.

"I became very ill," James recounts. "I was afraid I was going to die. The water was not clean. The vegetables were not clean. One African student died; many Americans were very ill. I was sick for a whole year. I became very thin and very weak."

"But I knew why I was there and I knew God had sent me. We prayed and I didn't give up."

James and Dorothy were at the seminary for four years. James received his Bachelor of Arts and Minister of Divinity degrees. Dorothy was awarded her Bachelors in Religious Education.

A day or so before the Halders left to go back to Bangladesh, they received a letter from Tom. He said, "The Gopalgonj church, Ghosherchar, is expecting you to come as their pastor."

"I didn't think much about it," James admits. "We were busy getting ready to leave the Philippines. By this time our little boy, Jose, was over a year old. We were trying to prepare him for traveling. I just folded the letter and put it in my pocket."

When the little family arrived in Dhaka, Tom met their flight. He repeated that Ghosherchar was expecting them. James and Tom worked out a date for the family to visit in Gopalgonj, but James refused to make a definate commitment. He knew village life would be difficult for Dorothy.

James met with his good friend, Dilip Datta, the secretary of the Bangladesh Baptist Fellowship. Dilip advised him to go to Gopalgonj for six months. James knew nothing could really be accomplished in that short time period. Both James and Dilip met with Tom. James agreed to go to Gopalgonj.

For Dorothy, it was hard. She was not familiar with village living. The uneducated people were foreign to her. Their behavior upset her. "Gopalgonj was not a friendly place then," James admits. But Dorothy made her way. She became involved in Ghosherchar.

"We have the best Sunday School in all of Bangladesh," Tom declares, "because Dorothy has worked so hard. If she accepts a responsibility, she does it. She and Gloria work very well together."

James adds, "When we came back to Bangladesh, I made a little salary, but God helped us to buy land, to build a house. Dorothy is happy. She can plant vegetables in her garden; we have fish from our pond. We have a little rice land. The Lord has blessed us and He has helped me to take care of my family. Matthew 6:33 has been so true for us. I pray that Jose, our son, will follow David and Philip. We will feel our ministry is a success if Jose loves the Lord."

James accepted the challenge at Ghosherchar and it became a good, strong mother church. James and Tom began church planting. James became an employee of the Bangladesh Baptist Mission in 1989. He is area evangelist for Gopalgonj district. Tom says, "He is the supervisor of our work, the leader of our team. The success story of Gopalgonj is James' success story."

James says, "Brother Tom is really my boss, but in their attitude Tom and Gloria are our elder brother and sister. The way we live our lives, they are examples to us. They have shown us how to love the Lord with all our hearts. They help us know the real meaning of life. We have learned it through their life and example."

There is no doubt, God sent Tom and Gloria to Gopalgonj. And then, God sent James and Dorothy.

Keeping My Father's House

Tom and Gloria decided long ago that their home would always belong to the Lord. Nobody would dispute that they have been true to that promise.

Listen to a few excerpts from letters home.

"We had a wonderful Christmas. Christa, my sister, and her two children have been visiting from Abu Dhabi for ten days. On Christmas day, we served a gallon-and-a-half of pink lemonade and 150 cups of tea, plus homemade sweets." (1974)

"The hotel business has not slowed down a bit. Within one week's time, we have had 31 extras at one meal or another. To top it all, our water pump has been out for a week and all of the water has to be bucketed in. But in all things give thanks, for we have a hand pump in the front yard, so we still have clean water close by." (1975)

"Gloria mixes up the drink mix and as the crowds continue to get bigger, she keeps weakening it down. The label is not correct. It will go much farther than the directions say." (1985)

"Our Christmas Eve celebration was a success—68 attended the tea, half Christian, half non-Christian. Everyone expressed appreciation for the home-baked goodies." (1991)

Early on, Gloria came to expect a steady stream of visitors daily. She also learned the proper Bengali behavior in serving them, and you must always serve a visitor.

You invite the visitor in, and you sit and talk awhile. You never ask immediately why they have come. After a time has passed, it is all right to say, "Did you have a special reason for coming, or did you just come to visit?" If they have a special reason, they will tell you. If they came only to visit, you serve them—hot tea, lemonade, a piece of cake or some other morsel. You never serve them as soon as they arrive; there must be time for proper socializing.

"I learned that early on in Faridpur," Gloria explains. "A young man came and I had just served some guests who had been there awhile. As soon as he sat down, I went to the kitchen and brought him something. He asked, 'Oh, do you want me to leave quickly?' When the others left, I asked him about his question. He explained that I needed to wait a little while before serving. Once people have been served, it means they are free to go."

Tom also has people come to his office frequently on Mission business or just to visit. He has a little office outside the Mission house in Gopalgonj. After he meets with his guests, he whistles and Gloria goes to the door.

"Can you do the needful?" he asks in English. Gloria knows that means can she serve them.

"I try to keep homemade cookies or a cake on hand all the time. In fact, I make a 13-by-9 cake almost everyday. It's always gone by the day's end. They love my cakes because there is very little good cake in Bangladesh. They even eat my failures. I've had plenty of failures because the electricity goes off when they are half-baked, and I have to finish the cake on the kerosene burner.

Tom says, "I've eaten a lot of delicious fallen cake. It makes good bread pudding, or sometimes Gloria covers it up with sauce. Either way, it is always eaten."

"When we go to Dhaka, I try to leave a cake in the freezer, because when we get back, the people start coming." Gloria says. "I try to buy some fruit that they don't have like apples and oranges while I'm in Dhaka. In a pinch I've even made pancakes. I can also make little doughnut puffs in a hurry."

"When the church council met recently, I expected 14 guests. I was surprised when 22 people came. I cut the cake into smaller pieces. I put a few slices of orange and some raisins on the plate and gave each a cup of hot tea."

Gloria tells about a little boy whose burned foot she had been treating for a week or so. "I gave him an apple after his last visit. It's been a long time since I've seen that much joy on a face. He grabbed the apple, rubbed it and polished it, and was still looking at it with delight as he went out the gate. I know the family situation. He had not had an apple in a long, long time."

The neighborhood children know when a stalk of bananas gets ripe. They appear at the gate and they eagerly accept one-third of a banana. The Thurmans planted a mulberry tree in the yard so that when the fruit falls, the children can come in, pick it up, and eat it.

Gloria explains why she does such things: "I read Baker James Cauthen's book, *Beyond the Call*. There is a chapter titled "Spread a Little Love." Dr. Cauthen mentions simple things we can do. It doesn't take a lot of effort to spread love. It means taking bananas to someone who doesn't have bananas, or a can of milk for a grandmother for her tea, or broccoli to a Muslim neighbor who has never had any. I want my sharing to be not just words, but also deeds."

And, do Tom and Gloria share their home! The people of the world have lodged under their roof! When they lived in Faridpur, their home was on the main road to the ferry. When the last ferry departed and people continued to come, the ferry man would say, "Go back to the Baptist Mission. They will let you spend the night."

So people came from England, Australia, Norway, New Zealand, India, and America to spend the night. During the war, Sydney Schanberg, then with *The New York Times*, Dan Coggin from *Time*, and a reporter from *The London Telegraph* were guests.

"Some of our favorite visitors were the Mississippi doctors who came after the war," Gloria says. "Dr. W. W. Walley and Dr. Van Landingham and his family blessed us as well as the Bengalis."

Another Mississippi duo that blessed the Thurmans, especially with laughter, were Marjean Patterson, the WMU executive director, and WMU executive board member, Sue Tatum. Tom had a new Bengali-made vehicle. The boys called it *muri tin* because it looked like the tin box that the puffed rice comes in.

"It was not a good vehicle," Gloria admits. "Sue and I were in the back seat, sweltering, waiting for the ferry. Tom mentioned something about how economical the *muri tin* was and Sue retorted, 'There is such a thing as false economy!'"

When Tom arrived at the next ferry, he reached to change gears and the whole gear shift came out in his hand! He finally decided to get rid of the *muri tin*.

Many Bangladeshis on their way to Dhaka or Khulna or any other point, have come to realize that they can find a place to rest at the Thurmans. Fellow missionaries, Foreign Mission Board staff members, and missionaries from other denominations—all who have come are welcomed. No one is turned away.

The most welcome guests of all, however, have been family members. Gloria's mother came after the war. Later, Gloria's brother, Will, came to visit.

"I had just completed two years as a journeyman in Kenya," Will tells. "I discovered upon my arrival that the brother-in-law, not the mother-in-law, is the 'villain' in Bangladesh. I was the subject of much ribbing. Had I come to check on my brother-in-law?"

Tom's sister, Louise, and her family came. Louise remembers they arrived in Dhaka shortly after Gloria's leprosy was diagnosed. "She met us at the airport with an enormous bandage on her leg. Later, she admitted that she didn't need even a Band-aid!"

Louise also recalls that they took a taxi from Dhaka to the first ferry. The floorboard was a piece of cardboard which fell out on the trip. "We held our feet up all the way to the ferry and watched the road rush by underneath us. It began to rain and the taxi had no windows. We opened two umbrellas to shield ourselves. The steering wheel had so much play, two complete turns were necessary for even a slight curve."

"When all the company comes" Gloria declares, "I have lots of help. In fact, I have household help all the time. It was an adjustment for me. People would be scandalized if we did not hire household help. It is expected, and they need the income, of course."

"We have wonderful helpers. Didi sweeps with a 20-inch broom and mops with a rag and towel. She also washes the dishes. Batul works in the yard and keeps the garden with a little short hoe. He also goes to the market for me. He brings the chicken home, kills it, and cleans it. The beef is brought home, thoroughly cleaned and ground by hand. Bosu is our night guard. Tom is gone so much, and I need someone to send if I need help. We depend on our Bengali helpers; we put our trust in them. They have never failed us. When we leave home, we leave our house key with them. When we come back, they have the house clean and ready for us. Even when we go home on furlough, we leave our key with our helpers."

"God has blessed us in this faraway land that is our home now. We are grateful that He has entrusted to us a wonderful house. He has given us help to run this house. We must share it with others. That is what keeping His house is all about."

Add a Pocketful of Elephant Ears

Bangladeshis love their food and are as proud of it as they are of their language. Tom and Gloria often tease each other before they go to a village to eat with the people.

"Do you think we will have a nice steak dinner?" Tom will ask Gloria. "Or maybe we'll have asparagus casserole!"

"No," Gloria will come back, "we'll have peach cobbler today. I can just taste it!"

Both of them know exactly what they will have to eat. The menu is the same every day of the year. No change, in any spices or any of the preparation, is ever considered.

Why don't we travel out to the village of Dattadanga for a nice lunch? We have been invited.

First, we take a rickshaw to the other side of Gopalgonj to catch a bus to the ferry to Dattadanga. The bus rattles and shakes along until we reach the ferry. It has already gone. No problem. We can hire a small country boat. We leap from the dock many feet down to the tiny boat. Miraculously, the boat does not capsize.

The boatman poles across the river and leaves his passengers to scramble up on the shore as best they can. A brisk walk through town brings us to another bus, more ancient than the first. After multiple attempts, it sputters to life, and we rattle down the potholed road. We reach the end of the bus line.

Not to worry, a flat-bed rickshaw hurries to our rescue. We climb on, laboriously, and we ride until the road rises, and then we hop off and push. Finally, we reach the path to the village and we walk into a joyful reception.

The cooking is already underway. The mud stoves are fired up. The stoves are built flat on the ground, usually outside the simple huts. The inside of the stove is completely covered with mud which has dried to a hard coating. The top, maybe 12 inches above the floor of the stove, is mud also. It has three openings, each about the size of a dinner plate. Pots sit on two of the holes. The third hole is the fuel hole. Dried branches, broken into small pieces, sticks, and dried cow dung patties are lit and fed into the hole. Soon the pots are bubbling. Children fetch more fuel as the women feed the fire and stir the pots.

Dal, the thick soup which is made of lentils and spices, is boiling. It looks like split-pea soup and is served as the first course over rice.

Vegetables are being prepared, so Gloria pulls out her pocket knife. "I always carry my pocket knife," she claims "I simply cannot use their long knives that they hold between their feet. If I used one of those knives, I would not have any vegetable left for the pot!"

The women pare the available vegetables: eggplant, potatoes, gourd, elephant ear bulbs—a delicacy. The vegetables are stir fried with lots of peppers, tumeric, and bay leaves. They are served as a second course, also over rice.

The third course is curry with fish. Since special guests are coming, a second curry with chicken is also being prepared. Fresh curry spices are ground for each meal. Tumeric, cumin, coriander, and red pepper are ground and mixed with the meat and enough water to make a gravy-like consistency. This, too, is served over rice.

No simple meal is being prepared at Dattadanga—a feast is being made. It is final examination day for the young men studying Theological Education by Extension. They and their teacher, Tom Thurman, are being honored.

The rice pot bubbles on another mud stove. The rice is dumped into a big basket—a Bengali sieve, it holds the rice and allows the water to drain through.

Lunch is ready. We doff our shoes and enter the little church. We sit cross-legged on the mats and are served rice and *dal*. One of the young preachers admonishes a guest of the Thurmans to roll up her sleeves. "You must eat the rice and *dal*, and let the *dal* run off your elbows!" They all laugh with delight. The young preachers do just that—eating with their right hands (only the right) they roll the rice into balls and raise it quickly to their mouths. *Dal* runs freely. Next came more rice and a covering of the curry and pepper-hot vegetables. The elephant ears are "brushy." But down they go, cleaning a path down the "innards."

Then comes another huge portion of rice lavished with chicken curry. Placed prominently on the plate of the foreigner, the guest of honor, is a sizeable fish head!

Gloria explains about the fish head. "The head is the best part, whether it's fish head, chicken head, or goat head. It is the prize piece of meat. Tom has said he could manage fish heads all right if they would remove the eyes. But when you look down and the fish is looking back at you, it's almost more than a body can take!"

Most days, people in the villages eat rice. Sometimes they have *dal* and a vegetable. Twice a month, they may have chicken or goat. There is usually some kind of fish available. People in the area of Gopalgonj have small ponds and they raise fish.

"This year, 1993, is a good rice year," Gloria says. "The people have more to eat than usual. Many, however, still go to bed hungry. In Dhaka you have to have money to buy food.

"If the people stayed in the villages, they would find something in the fields. Many in the cities are hungry, like those working in the garment factories."

Gloria adds that she and Tom are not hungry. "We may miss certain foods, but we have plenty to eat. In our homes, we missionaries prepare food that is much like the dishes you have at home."

When the Thurmans first came to Bangladesh, ready-made goods were not readily available. Gloria learned to make mayonnaise. "I'm not always successful, but I've learned to empty the 'failed' mayonnaise out of the blender and put another egg in and add the mayonnaise back gradually. It usually turns out all right the second time around. However, now I can buy a pint of American-made mayonnaise in Dhaka for $6.25. I splurge occasionally for sandwiches, but for salads or anything else, I still make my own mayonnaise."

Gloria makes catsup and mustard, using dry mustard and mixing it with vinegar or water.

"As a child, I helped with the canning, preparing vegetables, and washing jars," Gloria says. "I had never operated a pressure canner until I came to Bangladesh. The canner has been a life saver. We have our own garden, our own vegetables. From the market I can buy extra tomatoes and pineapple. I always put up lots of both of those."

"During rainy season, okra and eggplant are the only vegetables available. It really helps the okra and eggplant to add some tomatoes and onions," she says.

Chickens and ducks must be killed and cleaned before cooking. Fish must be cleaned and scaled.

Staples are not very "staple." Sifting the flour is a challenge. It must be sifted three or more times in rainy season, using a very fine sifter. Cream of wheat is available, but during rainy season it is nearly impossible to get rid of the tiny white bugs that infest it.

Learning to substitute is a way of life. "One of our favorite cakes is a Jello cake. I never have self-rising or cake flour, but I've learned to substitute," Gloria says. "I don't have buttermilk, but I add vinegar to powdered milk. One of the first things I do when we go to the States is buy a carton of fresh buttermilk. Tom and I drink it all."

"Having a sandwich for supper is not an easy supper. I must make the mayonnaise, make the bread, make something to go inside the sandwiches. If we have potato chips, I must cut thin, thin potato slices and stand over the skillet and cook them. It is no easy meal!"

"By and large, we have most anything we want. It just takes a little longer to prepare. People coming from the States keep us supplied with the one necessity of life for Tom—plenty of grits!"

Dinner is cooking on the three-hole mud stove.

90

The Bus Stops Here

Bangladeshi women rarely ride the bus, and they never ride alone. Foreign women certainly do not ride the bus—unless the foreign woman is Gloria Thurman. She rides quite often. "It always promises adventure!" she stoutly maintains.

However, it's not adventure that causes Gloria to ride the infamous Bengali buses, but necessity. For eight months, Gloria made two trips a month to Dhaka from Gopalgonj. These trips were necessary because she was entry and orientation coordinator for new Southern Baptist missionaries in the country. Even though Gloria made these trips alone, God always provided someone on each bus that she knew. In case help was needed, this was a blessing.

During dry months, the trips were made on private buses that carried the passengers to the big river. At the river, everybody boarded a motor launch to cross the river. On the other side, passengers climbed up the bank and walked down a sandy road to board the company bus again. Gloria was always loaded down with her suitcase and a bag of materials. Small boys were available to carry the bags, but the haggling over who would carry and the price of the carrying was always a problem.

If Gloria was fortunate enough to have a seat on the bus, she ended up holding someone's bag or someone's child on her lap so that the person could hold on to the bar as they stood in the aisle.

Bus terminals are another source of adventure. Buses don't have an assigned station, so passengers roam throughout the yards searching for their bus. Swarms of people look for their bus, and swarms of people are on hand just to watch. Woe to any woman in the crowd; many remarks are made at her expense. Of course, foreign women cannot understand, unless they are proficient in the language.

Gloria says, "Thanks goodness, Jim McKinley or James Young often took me to the Dhaka terminal, found my bus, and saw me safely on my way."

The terminal at Gopalgonj was never a problem. Most of the employees know the Thurmans personally. In fact, many come for tea at the Mission house which is practically next door to the terminal. So, few comments drift Gloria's way at Gopalgonj.

During the wet season, Gloria always goes by government bus. They cross the ferry with the passengers on board the bus. What a relief not to trudge with the luggage to reboard the bus! So why not go by government bus all the time? During dry season, waiting for the ferry would double the traveling time.

Another problem bus travelers face are breakdowns. Gloria was traveling from Magura, a city north of Gopalgonj, back home to Gopalgonj. Tom had carefully bought her a ticket on a through bus to within 23 miles of Gopalgonj. She was to change buses at that point and proceed home. Only 10 miles out of Magura, the bus "chucked" one time and came to a halt. The driver shook his head, ordered all passengers off the bus, and refunded their money.

"The driver assured us that he would help us board the next bus. Ha! People were literally hanging out the door of the next bus. Not one extra person could squeeze in. Another bus came along. Some of us hurried on. One mile, and the bus refused to go another inch."

"A third bus chugged up a little later. I found a place at the very back on the "woman's seat"—a long bench at the very end of the bus. A mother and her eight-year-old son were squashed in next to me. Actually, that one bus had a two-bus passenger load. There was no air. We were suffocating. Before long, the little boy became nauseated and baptized my right foot and the bottom of my sari!"

The bus finally reached Faridpur. By now it was so late, Gloria was afraid she would miss the last bus to Gopalgonj. To her relief, she heard two young men sitting near her discussing getting to the bus stand before the last bus left for Gopalgonj. She turned to them and said, "You can walk faster than I. Please tell the bus driver that the foreign lady from Gopalgonj is coming and ask him to wait."

The driver waited, and even kept a good seat for Gloria. She reached home by 9:30 that night. The trip had taken seven hours.

On May Day of 1990, Gloria and fellow missionary Betty Rains had tickets on a private bus to Gopalgonj. Tom and Randy Rains went early in the morning with their wives to the terminal to check on the schedule. They were told that May Day was a holiday and no buses would run that day.

Tom loaded Gloria and Betty in the van and off everybody went to the government bus stand. Half-way down Mirpur Road they met a government bus. Tom raised his hand signalling "stop." Miraculously, the bus stopped.

"Can you give seats to two women?" he asked as he pushed them on board the bus.

"We were on the bus and off it sped. I asked the destination of the bus. It was bound for a point far from Gopalgonj. However, it did go to the big river. Betty and I would get off the bus there and hope to find transportation to Faridpur and then on to Gopalgonj."

Unfortunately, when they reached the river there was no bus going to Faridpur. It turned out, however, that many passengers were trying to get to Faridpur, so a driver with a small bus was persuaded to take the passengers to the edge of Faridpur. He could not go into town for fear of the local bus lines that were on strike.

Fortunately, Gloria and Betty secured the services of a rickshaw and made the next leg of their trip into the city to the bus terminal.

"No bus to Gopalgonj today," the agent announced.

Back to the Baptist Mission in Faridpur the women traveled. They showered, changed saris, and went to a local restaurant for their one meal of the day. They spent the night at the Mission house.

Early the next morning, they boarded a local bus to the next ferry. After changing buses on the other side of the ferry, they finally made it to Gopalgonj around noon.

Only once has Gloria braved the night coach, and it seemed a necessity. The Mission meeting at Cox's Bazaar, way down south on the Bay of Bengal, had ended. Gloria wanted to stay over at the hospital there; one of the Mission evangelists had had an operation for leg injuries as a result of a motorcycle accident. Gloria wanted to spend some time with the young man and his wife.

Gloria had an airplane ticket from Cox's Bazaar to Dhaka. She left the hospital in plenty of time to catch her flight. However, at the airport, she was told that her flight was canceled and there was not another flight for two days. She was on stand-by for the later flight.

Off to the bus stand she went to find a bus to Chittagong, north of Cox's Bazaar. There was no longer a missionary that she knew in Chittagong. Gloria wondered where she could spend the night.

On arrival at the bus station, she was hopefull when she saw a bus that said, "Night Coach to Dhaka." Then Gloria noticed three women passengers already on the bus, and decided that was encouragement enough. She boarded the night coach, and after a long night's ride, she arrived in Dhaka the next morning.

Gloria says, "I was so thankful for safety, but I asked the Lord to deliver me from anymore night coaches!" She should have prayed, "Deliver me from night trips."

One Christmas Eve, 18 people spent the night in the little church at Dattadanga. Tom and Gloria were there along with their special guest, Leo Leake, from Columbia, Mississippi.

Leo got the small, hard wooden bed. The rest slept on mats on the mud floor. Christians who were close by came to spend the night so that the guests would not have fear.

Christmas was celebrated with carolers and then the church service. A love feast followed, then the trip home began. The first three miles were by flat-bed rickshaw, then a small bus took them to the river. A small boat across the river was followed by another bus ride. This bus was an old pickup truck converted into a small bus.

As sundown came, Gloria noticed that the bus driver did not turn on his lights. When she inquired about the lights, the driver told her he had no lights, but he knew the road.

"I knew the road, too," Gloria shudders, "and I knew there was one bridge that was just wide enough for one vehicle to cross, and the bridge had no sides."

Gloria quickly gave her two-battery flashlight to the bus helper. "Please get on the front bumper and use this light when we come to the bridge," she instructed.

"It's never boring," Gloria laughs. "Crossing the river on the launch, a young man sitting across the aisle asked, 'Madam, do you mind if I converse with you?' Then began the usual questions: 'How long have you been here?' 'Are you married?' 'How many children do you have?' 'How much is your salary?' 'What are your educational qualifications?' 'How do you like Bangladesh?'"

After answering the barrage of questions, Gloria opened a book and began to read. The young man said, "You have to excuse me, Madam. I don't often get to talk to such an exotic woman."

Dem Bones!

Gloria is master of the understatement. "We've had lots of broken bones," she says calmly as she begins the litany of accidents the Thurmans have endured.

Philip started it. During the war, when the Thurmans and McKinleys were staying in the Guest House in Dhaka, Philip, who was nearly six, fell off the wall surrounding the Guest House. Tom and Gloria took him to the Seventh Day Adventist Clinic; X-rays showed a broken arm. The doctors put it in a cast, and it mended quickly and completely.

The second loud crack happened in Faridpur. "We had what we call a *nor'wester*," Gloria explains. "It's a sudden storm that blows up from the northwest. You can never close all the windows before the rain gushes in. I always hurried to close the bedroom windows first so that the beds wouldn't get soaked. I was rushing down the hall to close the windows in the rest of the house. The bathroom window was still open and rain had blown into the hall. I hit the water and skidded, landing with one of my ankles buckled under me."

Gloria had terrific pain when she struggled to her feet. However, she also had guests. One of the Bengali preachers and Phil Parshall, a man from the International Christian Fellowship from Manikganj, a city near Dhaka, were spending the night with the Thurmans.

Gloria's accident occurred on the day before the Muslim festival *Eid* which signals the end of Ramadan, the month of fasting. Gloria's household helper, Ibrahim, a Muslim, had two days off.

Gloria endured, hobbling along, dragging her foot, and managed to get supper prepared. Then she slipped out and went to bed.

"I was miserable," she recounts, "but after taking several aspirin, I went to sleep. The next morning when I awoke, I thought, I cannot put my foot on the floor! It looked as big as my head; it was turning blue and it was throbbing. But the men wanted breakfast by six, so I got breakfast."

She noticed that when she propped her foot up, the throbbing lessened, so she propped and cooked. But when she walked she could hear a rubbing sound.

After the men left, Gloria told Tom, "I believe my foot is broken."

He replied, "Gloria, you know if your foot was broken, you couldn't be walking on it like you are."

"I say it's broken," she muttered.

By late morning, the pain had become unbearable and the swelling continued. Tom capitulated. "Let's go to the local hospital and have it X-rayed. Then we'll know for sure if it's broken."

They went to the hospital, but because it was *Eid*, nobody was working. Tom suggested going on to Dhaka.

Gloria said, "Tom, the ferry is probably not operating since it's *Eid*. Besides, six families have invited us to their *Eid* festivities. We should honor those invitations. Take the boys, and I'll stay home."

Tom decided that Gloria really needed to get to Dhaka. Gloria convinced him that she could go if Shova, her clinic helper, went with her. Reluctantly, Tom took Gloria and Shova to the ferry.

They waited several hours. The ferry man finally agreed to take one small load across the river if they'd pay a little extra.

Several taxis were on the Dhaka side of the river. Thirteen passengers piled into one taxi. "There were seven of us in the backseat," Gloria says. "Shova was sitting in my lap on my throbbing leg."

It was after dark before they reached Dhaka. Gloria called Missionaries Danny and Delores Hill who took her to Holy Family Hospital. Again there was no X-ray technician because it was *Eid*, but they did put on a partial cast to relieve the pressure.

"Come back tomorrow," they said.

After a restless night, Gloria went instead to the Orthopedic Hospital. X-rays showed the ankle was broken. Gloria insisted on a heel on the cast. "I'm too busy for crutches," she explained. They agreed to the heel if she'd use crutches until the cast was completely dry. She and Shova stayed in Dhaka for two days and then the Hills took them to the ferry.

"I hobbled onto the ferry with my crutches," says Gloria. "A local politician, the uncle of a friend, was on the ferry in his minivan. He said, 'You can't go to Faridpur on a bus like that!' A young man with him volunteered to take the bus and give me his place. So Shova and I got the backseat of the van and he brought me home."

96

Tom adds, "The people in Dhaka haven't forgiven me yet for sending Gloria off on a broken ankle!"

Next came Tom's turn. Shortly after the Thurmans moved to Gopalgonj, Tom was getting off the little motorized launch that brought him to the nearest landing. The water was not high enough to pull the boat in close, so Tom walked down the gang plank and then hopped onto a date tree that was in the water. The date tree was slick. Tom fell and landed on his foot. He hobbled up the bank and had to be helped into a rickshaw. He went straight to the doctor in Gopalgonj. Fortunately, it was not *Eid*, so he was promptly X-rayed and "plastered."

Tom says, "It was the hot, hot, muggy season and my foot felt scalded. I'd push a coat hanger inside the cast and scratch."

Gloria joins in, "He kept saying that the skin had rotted off, it was decayed to the very bone. So I took him back to the hospital and they cut a little window at the very spot Tom indicated. To his amazement, the flesh was perfectly sound. He decided he could live with that cast the rest of the six weeks."

His broken leg cannot compare to what will always be called in Bangladesh: "Tom's accident," or as Gloria calls it "the nightmare."

Tom was out in the villages and the rain was torrential. On his way home, a man stopped the bus. One of the main bridges between Faridpur and Gopalgonj was flooded. Tom leaped off the bus and started across the bridge, and one of the sides collapsed. He hurriedly retraced his steps.

One of the men took a bamboo pole and placed it over the bridge. Bus passengers would hold onto the pole and cross over, then they had to walk a mile to catch another bus.

Tom took a hot shower, changed clothes, and ate a good meal. Then he took off in the rain to attend a camp program being held in another part of the area.

That night, after nine o'clock, a police truck came to the Thurman's front gate. The Mission vehicle and the Mission driver, Khaleque, were on the other side of the broken bridge with a load of baby ducks for Gopalgonj. By this time, a double-pole bamboo bridge as well as a bamboo rail had been put across the river. However, Gloria decided not to strike out in the dark and try to transport ducks across that bridge. She sent word to Khaleque to stay put. Mr. Thurman would be home in the morning and they would come then for the ducks.

The next morning, Tom and David went to the bridge. They managed to get the ducks across the bamboo bridge and into the van. About two miles from home, a bus stopped, causing the van to pull around the bus. When Tom saw how close they were to the bus, without thinking, he put his hand out—to move the bus over.

His hand hit the bus with such force that it broke the big bone, the radius, in his left arm, and dislocated his wrist. People on the bus heard the bone crack. Tom blacked out. David drove home quickly.

"When I saw Tom's face, I was scared to death," Gloria recalls.

They got Tom inside and Gloria tried to elevate his arm. He passed out again from the pain. She sent Bosu, the night guard, to get Dr. Saha, the Hindu doctor. He came immediately and fixed a partial cast for Tom's arm.

Now, how to get to Dhaka? "Lord, give me wisdom," Gloria whispered. And He did. They had gotten a telephone in Gopalgonj but could never get through. Gloria called Faridpur and a Christian man answered. Gloria said, "Please send someone to the Gopalgonj-Faridpur crossroads. The Mission vehicle should be coming soon. Stop the vehicle and tell Khaleque that Mr. Thurman has a broken arm. Please come back to the broken bridge and wait."

Gloria also got through to Dhaka immediately and asked the McKinleys to wait up and not lock them out.

Sixty of the church people had gathered at the house. It was pouring rain, but they all wanted to help. James Halder and Subash Bhowmik went with the Thurmans to the bridge.

Gloria admits she was really afraid when she saw the high bridge and strong current. She and David had suitcases to carry, but the real problem was for Tom to go across. He had to catch the pole with his opposite arm, because the arm next to the pole was the broken one. Tom slid his feet along the bamboo. "God was good," Tom says, another classic understatement from the Thurmans.

A weary Khaleque was on the other side. Tom said, "I know how tired you must be."

Khaleque said, "Sir, I was so tired, but when I heard about your condition, my tiredness left."

They made it into Dhaka after midnight. The next morning after X-rays confirmed the bad break, the Bengali doctor put in a steel plate with six screws.

"The ordeal was not over," Gloria says. "The stay in the hospital that night nearly did me in. The man in the bed next to Tom kept complaining of itching, stinging, and burning. He had a cast on up to his waist. Coming out of that cast were maggots. They were crawling on the bed sheet, falling on the floor."

"When David and Jim McKinley arrived, I told them of the conditions. It took less than two hours for those two to have Tom checked out of the hospital."

Tom and Gloria stayed at the McKinleys until Tom was able to travel. They asked the doctor to come there to check on him.

In February 1980, the Thurmans were in Faridpur for the annual meeting of the Bangladesh Baptist Fellowship. About midnight, Gloria awoke with her left shoulder in excruciating pain. She took eight aspirins in one hour with no relief. She says, "I sat and sobbed, the pain was so intense. I didn't lie down the rest of the night."

By morning, her right wrist had swollen to twice its size and she couldn't move her fingers. Tom took her to the Presbyterian Clinic.

There were no broken bones this time; the doctor diagnosed arthritis. He wrapped her hand and put it in a sling. She was to experiment to see if it was best mobile or immobile. Also, the doctor prescribed massive doses of aspirin to reduce inflammation.

For about four years Gloria took as many as 24 aspirins a day. It kept the swelling down and helped her endure the pain.

Under extreme interrogation, Gloria admits she's never without pain. "But I have learned to live with it," she replies.

In 1990, Gloria decided that that much aspirin was not good for her. She asked the Lord to help her do without. "Unless the pain is severe in my spine or shoulder, I never take aspirin now," she says.

"I know my bones are becoming harder and stiffer, but that's part of it. They are not drawn."

Even when aching, dem bones serve   and serve—and serve.

David and Philip, with his arm in a cast.

Laugh and the Mission Laughs with You

"At a Mission meeting in Bangladesh, the missionaries' kids gave their "Aunt" Gloria the award for sharing bad news the quickest of anybody," laughs fellow Missionary Guinevere Young. Then James and Guinevere tell the story that has caused Gloria untold teasing.

"I simply tell things like they are," Gloria says in her own defense. "That is so foreign to Bengali culture. I have a hard time adjusting to the culture in this matter. If I know something and somebody asks me about it, I tell them."

The Mission says, "If you want something told, tell Gloria!"

Gloria went to Rajbari with Tom to visit the pastor at his home. His daughter-in-law was from Gopalgonj. After Tom and Gloria had visited with the pastor, the daughter-in-law came out. She turned to Gloria and asked, "Auntie, do you know a man in Gopalgonj named Mohendro Babu?"

Gloria told her that she had known him for a long time.

She asked, "Do you know about his son-in-law, the one who has been sick in the hospital in Dhaka?"

"Yes, I know about him," Gloria said.

"Do you know the last report on him?" the girl pursued.

Gloria said, "He died last week."

When Gloria said that, the girl threw her arms back and hit the floor! She started rolling and moaning. She rolled off the porch and into the yard.

"The father-in-law could have killed me," Gloria recalls. "I was innocent! I asked the father-in-law what the girl's interest was in the young man. He was her brother!"

The father-in-law had gotten the message saying her brother had died, but he hadn't told her. He was waiting for his son to get home so that he could carry his wife home to be with her family. The loud-mouthed missionary had calmly announced the news.

Gloria moans, "By this time everybody in Rajbari had come to see what was wrong. I grabbed the young woman and begged her to come inside as the crowd got bigger and bigger. I was so glad to leave that place and go home. I've never been back to that house. Of course, they probably wouldn't let me back inside!"

Tom told the story to missionary friends in Dhaka and now it is part of Mission history.

Gloria has had several "baptizing" incidents that are also part of Mission lore. The first happened when the Thurmans moved to Gopalgonj. The last 23 miles were covered by motor launch. It took nearly six hours to make the trip with seven stops along the way.

"We were coming from Dhaka. Philip was coming home from boarding school. Tom and both boys had big suitcases," Gloria remembers. "As we got off the bus at the river, we saw the launch was ready to go. We got in a little country boat and headed for the launch. Tom waved his arms to let them know we were coming."

When they reached the launch, Tom and the boys caught hold of the window and swung their long legs first to the window and then to the top deck, hauling the heavy suitcases up as they went.

Gloria snorts, "Then the clumsy woman in her sari tried to pull up to the window. I did catch hold, but I couldn't step that high. I started to go back in the boat, but the boatman, thinking I was already on the launch, had pulled away. I hung on to the window, but from the waist down, I was dangling in the water. The launch motor started! There was no sign of Tom, Philip, or David."

Finally, one of the Bengali men happened to look over the side of the boat. He found Tom and stuttered, "A foreign lady, I think it may be your wife, is hanging in the water!"

Tom looked over the ledge at Gloria and she said, "Don't worry about me. Go ahead and get the suitcases up!"

One of the men and Tom pulled Gloria out of the water. Everybody watched the foreign woman being hauled in.

"My family never ever again bounded on a boat without giving me special attention!" says Gloria.

Gloria was accompanied on another baptism. During rainy season a boat carries church members in Gopalgonj across the little river between the road and church. Dilip Datta, who was teaching the January Bible study, another worker, Tom and Gloria had reached the other side. The worker hurriedly jumped off the end of the boat, tipping it so that water rushed in. Dilip, Tom, Gloria, and the boatman just stood in the boat until it went all the way down. Fortunately, it was a shallow spot near the bank, so they were only waist deep in the water. Somebody finally handed them a bamboo pole so they could hold on and scramble to safety.

Gloria endured a third baptizing solo. She claims it was the most humiliating of all her "water" experiences. She was in Dhaka for a HEED language school meeting. HEED stands for Health, Education, Economic Development, a para-church organization in Bangladesh. Gloria serves on the language board.

The streets of Dhaka were flooded. On Mirpur Road, right in front of the Guest House, the water was swirling. Gloria got out of a baby taxi and a boatman came to ferry her the short distance to the Guest House. The bit of land in front of the Guest House was being purchased by someone, so a low boundary wall had been built.

The boatman said, "Madam, I will take you to the boundary wall. If you step out the left side of the boat, you will be standing on the wall, only ankle deep in the water. Walk down the wall and you'll reach the Guest House gate."

Gloria carefully put her foot over the left side of the boat and touched something solid, but when she took a very small second step, she went completely under the water. The boatman shoved the boat away, or she would have come up under the boat. He was embarrassed; Gloria was drenched!

"I got hold of the side of the boat and the boatman towed me to the gate. I lost a shoe which the boatman later found in all that filthy water," Gloria says.

"Another missionary group was meeting at the Guest House. Thankfully, they were in meetings and missed seeing me slosh in! I took a long shower and then a bath. The water was filled with sewage and filth. The experience makes me shudder to this day!"

Tom says that you don't have to be crazy to live in Bangladesh, but it helps. Gloria adds, "The Lord has a good sense of humor. Some of the things I've been caught in, He had to be laughing."

Gloria tells how she, Didi, her household helper, and Dorothy Halder were invited to a Hindu neighbor's house. The man had built the Thurmans' house and the office/schoolroom outside their house. Tom had worked with him in a food-for-work project so that he could cut a pond. He had stocked it with fish and he wanted them to come for a fish dinner.

The invitation was for ten in the morning. They got there on time and the neighbor wasn't there. His wife gave them *muri* and brown sugar and they ate and talked for an hour.

Then the husband came with a bucket of fish and said, "Enjoy yourselves. I must go back to work." Off he went.

They sat and the bucket of fish sat. Gloria asked Didi, "Are we to take these fish home or what? We can't sit here all day."

Didi told the wife that they were going.

"Oh, no," the wife replied, "you are to eat with us. The children's father has caught the fish." She went into the house and came out with rice, lentils, and spices. She put them down in front of Gloria, Didi, and Dorothy and said, "Ladies, here it is."

"We got busy," Gloria states. "We cleaned and cooked the fish. The wife and children came when it was ready and ate with us."

"After that, when anybody asks us to come eat fish, I always ask them what time it will be cooked and ready," Gloria laughs.

Another funny experience occurred when the Thurmans were going to Ghilatolah, a new village church. Tom had been there several times, but it was Gloria's first visit. They crossed the river in a sampan boat, then were going down a long dusty road in a rickshaw. Subash Bhowmik, the area evangelist in Magura was in front of the Thurmans in another rickshaw.

A rickshaw man coming from the opposite direction got even with Tom and Gloria, he looked up at them and screamed in a loud voice, "What in the world is it?" and pedaled away as quickly as possible! Subash will never let the Thurmans forget that encounter.

A band had met them when they got off the boat and played them into the village. There were three chairs ready for Subash, Tom, and Gloria. Hordes of people surrounded Gloria as she sat. They stared intently at her.

"Finally, I noticed a small house directly behind us," Gloria says "I got up, went to the woman in front of the house and asked her if I could come in. I said to her that I knew it was not their custom for men to stare at women in such a way. She took me in. When men would come to the door and look inside, she would tell them, 'A woman is here.' So she protected me all that day."

When night came, Tom and Gloria were prepared a sleeping place on the front porch. The people put down mats. The Thurmans put down bed rolls and put up mosquito nets.

"About 11 o'clock, I saw flashlights blinking down the road," Gloria says. "I said to Tom that 'new lookers' are coming. Don't you dare greet them. Be quiet. Stay under the covers. If they haven't seen by now, they can come tomorrow."

The Thurmans turned their backs to the road. The people came to the edge of the porch, shining their lights on the foreigners. One

104

of them grumbled, "It looks like they've gone to bed. We'll have to come back tomorrow." And they did!

Tom and Gloria have laughed at many things that have happened with her clinic practice. Even on the road her skills are called upon. Once she was traveling from Faridpur to Dhaka with Journeyman Marlin Harris and his mother, Kate.

As Marlin drove on the ferry, a man who had been standing at the edge of the ferry entrance came to the car door. He said to Marlin, "You ran over my foot!"

Marlin said, "Sir, you should have gotten your foot off the road."

Gloria quickly jumped out of the car and took out her cosmetic kit. All she could find was concentrated shampoo and a Band-aid.

With great "skill," Gloria cleaned the man's scrapped toe and applied the Band-aid. The patient went away greatly relieved.

One Saturday before Easter, just before dark, the young people came running to the Thurmans' house. They were in charge of the Sunrise Service for the whole community the next day. They had forgotten one thing. They needed an angel.

"Would you be the angel, Auntie?" they chorused.

Gloria sputtered, "But I don't know what to say . . . "

"You don't have to say anything," they interrupted, "just wear a white sari and a pair of wings and hold your arms outstretched!"

Gloria's protests fell on deaf ears so she fashioned wings from an old bedsheet and some clothesline, made a Christmas tinsel wreath for her head and ironed a fresh white sari for her heavenly robe.

"I finally decided that might be my one and only chance to be an angel," she reasoned. "I might as well take advantage of it!"

And she laughed.

Laugh and Bangladesh laughs with you. 1983 workshop in Dhaka.

"My best work has been with the women and children," says Gloria.

I Take Thee, My Mother-in-law!

The romantic Western conception of love and marriage is boy meets girl, boy and girl fall in love, get married, and live happily ever after in their own rose-covered cottage.

The Bengali conception of love and marriage is a bit different: uncle or older brother finds suitable girl and visits girl's family. If all demands are met by both sides of each family, marriage takes place, and the girl comes to live with her mother-in-law (and husband) ever after. Sometimes, even happily!

Weddings are still arranged in Bangladesh. And the unbelievable process above is really true:

1. Uncle or older brother finds suitable girl. This is a search that begins early, often at birth. Many suggestions are made. Many questions are asked.

2. They visit the girl's family. They sit and talk. They want to know the family background, what their income is, what their family situation is. They talk to the girl, asking simple questions at first and then a few tricky ones to see how she reacts.

3. More visits follow. If all is satisfactory, representatives from both families meet with their list of demands.

4. Every family has demands. Some have outrageous demands. The groom's family usually demands a certain amount of money, a bicycle or motorcycle, a radio or television, a watch, some land.

The bride's family also outfits the groom. The average village groom wears what looks like a pajama suit: white pants with a drawstring waist and a long white shirt that's worn outside. However, in the town or city, the groom wears a three piece suit.

The bride's family makes many demands as well. The bride asks for gold: a nose piece, earrings, and bracelets. The gold becomes the new family's bank account and security. If the groom's family is poor, she may only receive the gold nose piece for her pierced nose.

They also ask for the bride's trousseau. Recently Gloria had an unusual experience in regard to a bride's trousseau. When she arrived on the day of the wedding, the sister-in-law of the bride came in with a small trunk and its key. She said to Gloria, "You are the guard for the possessions today."

Gloria asked, "Do I have to sit here with the trunk all day?"

"No," the sister-in-law answered, "Someone will guard the trunk, but you'll be the one to open it and give the contents out."

The sister-in-law gave Gloria a list of everything in the trunk that the groom's family had provided for the bride. As the bathing ceremony began, women started coming and asking for different articles. Gloria unlocked the trunk, gave the article, and put a check mark on the list. When an article was returned, she checked again. Inside the trunk were: a comb, hair ribbons, bobby pins, barrettes, mirror, soap in a soap case, powder, lipstick, cream, colored circles for the forehead, nail polish, the red wedding sari, blouse, petticoat, bra, sandals, bracelets, earrings, nose piece (gold), the rings for the bride and groom, a sari for the bride's mother, and a sari for the bride's aunt (or other relative) who was to accompany the bride on the honeymoon. Of course, the honeymoon was going to the groom's house, but the aunt went also and stayed for ten days.

5. The marriage takes place. But first, the groom is bathed by the groom's party at his house. Likewise, the bride is bathed at her house. Anybody who is anybody in the community takes part in the bathing ceremony. They grind spices and rub them on the bride and groom. Then they are taken to separate ponds where the spices are washed away. Then they are dressed for the wedding.

The vows are exchanged. Muslim and Hindu ceremonies are in the home. Christians are married in the church.

After the ceremony everyone goes to the bride's house for the wedding feast. After the feast is over, the groom, bride, and aunt go to the groom's house. The next day, the groom's feast is held.

6. The bride is now a daughter-in-law in the house of her in-laws. She visits her parent's house once a year or on special occasions.

Tom and Gloria are active participants in the weddings. A mother of a bride-to-be came to Gloria when they lived in Faridpur. The bride's family was to provide her sari and the groom's family was to provide his outfit. The mother explained they didn't have the money for the sari, about $5. Gloria bought the sari. The bride married Bosu, who is now the Thurman's night guard in Gopalgonj.

"That's not the only sari we've furnished," Gloria says. "In fact, Philip and David ride their dad pretty hard on his wedding activities. We'll be invited to a wedding and the boys will ask Tom how much he has in that rice pot!"

"But I've found my place at the wedding feasts," Gloria explains. "I wash dishes. There are never enough dishes and they've found I'm a good dishwasher. The dishes are cleaner because I use soap powder and insist on hot water!"

Sometimes, however, Gloria plays a bigger part than being the dishwasher. "The first time I had an active role in helping to arrange a wedding," Gloria recalls, "was with my dear friend, Anima, when we lived in Faridpur."

Anima was past the eligible age to get married. Years before, she had wanted to marry a young man in Faridpur, but her aunt had spoken against it. Most thought she'd never marry.

Anima's older brother came to Gloria and said, "If anybody can convince Anima to get married, it's you."

He told Gloria about the man they were considering who was a school teacher as was Anima. He also told her that he would send Anima to the Thurman house the next afternoon.

Anima came and they chatted and drank tea and ate cake. Then Gloria said, "What you think about your future? Before long, your mother and father won't be here and you'll be left by yourself."

Anima said, "I'll just continue teaching. What future do I have?"

"If you had a chance to change your future," Gloria asked, "would you be willing?"

"Like what?" she questioned

"Like becoming a wife," said Gloria.

Anima burst into tears. She sobbed for at least 15 minutes. Gloria could not get her to stop. She said, "Anima, it's time to stop crying and think about this."

Anima stopped a minute, and then she started sobbing again.

Gloria chided, "You are beside yourself. If you're not willing to talk about it, tell me. There is no pressure. This will not affect our friendship in any way, but I need to know how you feel."

A new outburst of sobs! Gloria kept talking, "I will not speak of this again. I'm going into the kitchen to work. When you decide you can get up and go home, you go."

In a few minutes, Anima asked Gloria to come back in. She began to ask questions about the man and where he lived. Finally, she said, "Well, if you and my brother think it's the right thing for me, what else can I do!" A new flood of tears!

"Does that mean I have your permission to tell your brother you are willing for him to talk to the man?" Gloria inquired.

"Go tell him," Anima sobbed.

That night the brother came and he and Gloria worked out the details. Right after Christmas, Anima became a wife. And she did live happily ever after.

Another wedding Gloria had a lot to do with was for a young man in Faridpur and a Gopalgonj girl. Tom Kirkpatrick, a fellow missionary in Faridpur, was a friend of the young man, Rupak Saha. He knew Rupak had made many trips to Gopalgonj, and he always had a meal with a particular family who had a daughter named Koci.

On one trip to Gopalgonj, Rupak visited Gloria and confessed, "Koci and I have prayed for three years that we will be married because we love each other. God has told us to tell you. My father, my auntie, and my brothers love you. They will listen to you."

Gloria takes up the story, "They wanted me to work two ways: I was to talk to Koci's family in Gopalgonj. Then I was to go to Faridpur and talk to Rupak's family."

So, Gloria talked to Koci's family. "I never got a positive answer from them," she recalls. "It wasn't negative, it just wasn't positive. I found out later they had someone else in mind for her."

After a long talk with Koci, Gloria was assured that Koci was interested and willing. So she decided to travel to Faridpur to see the reaction of Rupak's family.

"The only reason I could think of that his parents might object to the marriage was the girl was from a broken home. The mother had left the father and the children. The mother had remarried a non-Christian. This was a real problem."

Gloria talked to Rupak's mother first. The mother mentioned the broken home. She also said the final decision would rest with the older son. They set a time that night for Gloria to talk with him.

"The older brother came that night and we talked," Gloria sighs. "Finally, I said that it was after 11 o'clock; we had talked enough."

In desperation Gloria said, "Older brother, I am simply not accustomed to all of this. I don't know what else is necessary, but I'm telling you now, I am leaving on the 7 o'clock bus in the morning. If someone from your family has not come with an affirmative answer, I will assume your answer is no. I will return to Gopalgonj and I will never again discuss this matter with you!"

The next morning, the older brother went to Gloria and said, "Ask the representatives of the girl's family to come to our home in Faridpur and we will talk with them. Rupak has said that we don't have to arrange this wedding, but if we don't, we are not to think of arranging any other for him. I think he means it."

The wedding took place, and Koci has won a place in her mother-in-law's heart as well as the heart of the older brother.

"They have three precious children now," Gloria says proudly. "All of them call me grandma!"

Wedding of David and Lipika Boiragee in 1988 in Dhaka.

The Weeping Prophetess

Tom has said many times that Gloria will never have an ulcer. "She won't," he declares. "If you weep, you don't get ulcers, and Gloria does weep! She's the weeping prophetess."

"Sometimes all we can do is care and touch," he explains. "Gloria sits with the women and they pour out their troubles. Many, many times I've come in and found her with several women, and they are all weeping. The women get up saying they feel better now. They can go back and face life. Somebody knows their plight and weeps with them. Now they can hope. They are people of hope."

Many times Gloria has penned her grief or concern in personal notes to friends in the States. Again and again she begins, "You would weep . . . " as she chronicles a family in distress, a dying child, a nation torn by war, a devastating physical disaster. And the reader knows she has wept. But never for herself. "She never complains" is heard over and over. Personal distress she takes to the Father silently. But she cries for the children.

Gloria remembers a time she was called out in the night. "I should go," Gloria whispered to Tom. "The girl is from a fairly new Christian family. Her mother is not with her."

She quickly wrapped a sari around herself and called the night guard to accompany her. They walked to the village, fording two small streams to reach it.

Going into the dark hut, Gloria found the doctor's assistant working on the young woman. She was having frequent seizures. A drip had been started in her arm. Two women were anchoring the arm as she writhed in pain and convulsions.

After a long pain-filled hour, Gloria realized the patient's physical strength was ebbing. There was no sign of consciousness.

Gloria sent a note to the doctor requesting that he come at once. He did. He worked for over an hour with the young woman.

Finally, he shook his head and turned to Gloria, "The only hope I see is a forceps delivery. Maybe we can save the mother."

"Then please do so," Gloria begged.

"With your permission, I will do it," the doctor replied.

He brought out a baby boy who had evidently been dead quite some time. In silence, several of the women wiped the tears as they cleaned up the little hut. They wrapped the little body and laid it on the corner of a straw mat.

The doctor worked for almost another hour to be sure the mother's blood pressure and vital signs were stabilizing.

As the sun rose, Gloria lined a little apple crate coffin and tenderly placed the little body inside. She started the long walk home, trying to cover the blood stains on her sari as people peered at her.

And she cried.

"When we lived in Faridpur and the clinic was operating full-speed, a woman came to the clinic with her child. He was infested with worms and no telling what else," Gloria says.

The child was a little boy, small, perhaps three years old. The mother gave the boy to Gloria and pleaded, "Please do something."

"I realized as I looked at the child that he was almost gone. I knew there was nothing I could do. I put the child back in the mother's arms and wrote a note to the Muslim doctor, Dr. Zahid."

Within 30 minutes they returned, giving Gloria a note from Dr. Zahid saying, "Too late." She pitched the child into Gloria's arms.

"I realized the backbone was already getting stiff," Gloria says, dabbing at flowing tears. "He was gone."

Gloria went on her back porch and laid the child down on a small table. The mother peered in, realizing the child had died. She fell down in hysterics on the floor. Her mother-in-law was with her. Gloria asked her to comfort and control the mother.

She went into her medical storeroom and brought out half of an old white sheet. She wrapped the little body as the Bengalis do for burial. She handed the child to the mother-in-law who reached down and caught her daughter-in-law by the hand.

"Let's go home now," she said softly. "Where else could you have gotten such care and burial clothes as well?"

As they crept out, bearing the tiny burden, Gloria's heart ached, and she wiped away her tears.

A time of intense personal tragedy concerned the Thurman's dear friend, Mavis Pate. When Tom and Gloria arrived in East Pakistan in

1965, an immediate bonding took place. Mavis said, "Perhaps the friendship came naturally because of a shared love for country cooking and cornbread dressing!"

The Mission had filed a formal petition to the government in 1964 for permission to build a hospital. Permission was never granted. The doctors and nurses who had come to staff that hospital were frustrated beyond measure. They were not allowed to practice medicine in the midst of overwhelming need.

Tom says, "Mavis struggled with the dreams being thwarted, but she kept busy. She managed the Guest House. She worked in a social service setting. But she was not nursing, and it was a struggle. We understood the struggle since we had waited nearly two years for a visa. We sympathized and we listened a lot."

Mavis wrote in her diary more than once, "I found, as usual, that Gloria is my most patient and understanding sounding board. . . ."

Tom adds, "Mavis took such pride in Gloria's little bush clinic. She saw Gloria doing what she herself wanted to do, but couldn't because she didn't have registration. On her last trip to Faridpur, she gave Gloria her medical books, the Merck Manuals. Mavis said, 'When you come upon this problem, this is what you do.'"

Gloria continues, "Mavis loved our boys. She was there for the birth of both Philip and David. Ray Register, who wrote her biography, *Clothed in White*, said that her diary is full of comments about our boys. She looked upon them as her children."

"On furlough in 1969, we went to see Mavis in her hometown of Ringgold, Louisiana. She, too, was on furlough. We stopped and bought a dozen roses. Philip gave them to his 'Aunt' Mavis. She never forgot that her little whiteheaded boy brought her roses."

Also, in 1969, a call came to Mavis to fill the position of operating room nurse at the Southern Baptist Hospital in Gaza. Tom and Gloria, Jim McKinley, and Bill Marshall, who was the field representative for the Foreign Mission Board in the Middle East, spent long and agonizing hours talking and praying with Mavis. The decision was made; on February 13, 1970, Mavis headed to Gaza.

Tom continues, "We heard on the Voice of America that an American nurse from Ringgold, Louisiana, had been shot. The name was garbled, but we knew it was Mavis. It was January 1972."

Gloria adds, "We went home on furlough in 1973 by way of Gaza to visit Mavis' grave. Her parents met us at the grave site and we had a small memorial service. After her parents left, Tom and I stayed to have a quiet time alone."

They said good-bye. And both of them wept.

Danger is no stranger to the Thurmans. However, God has protected. "We have felt that wonderful protection," Gloria says. "And we weep with joy when protection comes from unlikely places."

One night after the Thurmans had moved to their new house in Gopalgonj, they had gone to bed and drifted off to sleep. Then Gloria heard talking at the gate. Curious, she went to stand at the door. She heard the night guard talking to some men. He took the key, unlocked the gate, and the men came in.

"Bosu," Gloria called, "what is this?"

One of the men, a neighbor, answered, "*Masi ma* (Auntie), we are here. You go back to sleep. We are going to stay here all night."

"Why? What on earth is wrong?" she inquired.

Another neighbor replied, "There are two boatloads of people coming up the river. We understand they know about your house. We aren't sure what they have in mind, so we've come to guard your house. It's going to be all right."

Gloria's voice trembles, "Four men—one Christian and three Hindus—had left their families and they stayed until daybreak."

Another anxious time when God used unlikely people was during the Gulf War. Tom wrote home about the strong anti-American sentiment in the country. The local police called to advise the Thurmans to keep a low profile.

Tom says, "On Saturday night, January 19, 1991, a procession came down the road headed for our house. Several hundred were shouting, "Down with Bush." They were turned back at the bus terminal which is only 300 yards from our house. We have been neighborly. The drivers would come to use our phone. Gloria has always treated them well; she served a lot of tea and sweets.

"The bus terminal leaders told the group that the Thurman family had nothing to do with the war. We had lived here a long time in peace and they could not pass the bus stand to get to us. The group turned and went back to the city.

"Friday at noontime is the weekly prayer time for Muslims. It was reported that after prayers on January 26, 1991, they would march to our house. At 12:30, six policemen showed at our gate. One had a machine gun and four had regular rifles. They stayed about an hour and drank tea and ate cake. Then they went to the bus stand and stayed there another two hours."

Later the Thurmans heard that a Muslim leader who had gotten one of their tube wells stood in the meeting and pled for reason.

Gloria says, "So many people were good to us during these hard days. God's goodness never fails." And a tear trickled down her face.

116

Bangladeshis Speak

The tremendous love the Thurmans have for the people of Bangladesh is unquestioned. For nearly three decades, since 1965, their love and their lives have been poured out for Bengal.

Simon Sicar, the president of the College of Christian Theology of Bangladesh says, "I am sure someday at the throne of God, many Bangladeshis will say, 'I have known the great love of Jesus Christ through the love of Tom and Gloria Thurman. That is why I am here at the throne of God.' "

Simon, the great, great, great grandson of that long-awaited convert of William Carey, is a long time friend of the Thurmans. He reminisces, "When Tom and Gloria first came to East Pakistan, they were a young couple. I was privileged to teach them the language. I was then the language teacher for the Southern Baptist Mission.

"Both Tom and Gloria have a tremendous love for the Lord," he continues. "That love is expressed in their relationship with other people. You go to their home, even after midnight or very early in the morning, and you are welcome. No one is turned away."

Simon explains that many call Gloria "Ma," mother. "I have not known another missionary called "Ma." She is an exception. It doesn't come from one day's relationship. "Ma" is the one who gives love; she does not think of receiving.

"Gloria has gone through many physical problems. Nobody understands that because she never talks about it, never complains. Someone comes to her with a problem not so big as her own, yet she opens her heart, extends her arms, and assists them in anyway she can. This is what we have seen."

Simon points out that Gopalgonj used to be a barren area. Tom and Gloria went there and shared their hearts, showed their love.

Now a large number of churches are in the Gopalgonj area. The mother church, Ghoserchar, had become a powerhouse.

He tells how Tom and Gloria have a simple life, how both of them travel by bus. "Tom takes Bibles and tracts that he gives out as he travels. He's put thousands of Bibles in the hands of the people.

Simon also speaks of Gloria's clinics. "Why does she do that? She thinks this is something she can do for the people and maybe then she can get in their hearts and witness to them. If there is no medical need, she will give to others eggs, a tin of coffee, some fruit. It means she has thought about them. She loves them.

"I must tell how Tom and Gloria loved the freedom fighters of our country. The Thurmans and McKinleys stayed during the time of the civil war. There was terrible bloodshed. They could have left. But they loved us so deeply. Some of us came with our families to the Guest House to stay for protection during the December siege. They said, 'Do not be afraid. We are with you.' They were our shepherds taking care of us.

"I remember Gloria standing at the gate with a broken heart as the people streamed by. It gave heart to those people. 'The missionaries are still here. They are with us!'

"Why did they not leave? It was because they loved us and were willing to suffer with us. It was not a simple love, but deep-rooted love that risked their very lives.

"Recently, I was at their house. Every morning very early there is prayer meeting there. I did not get up for the prayer meeting. They do so every morning. It is tremendous faithfulness to the Lord to get up early and then work so late at night.

"There will be many tears shed when Gloria leaves Bangladesh. The gap that will be created when she is gone, nobody can fill. I am glad for a book about Gloria. But it is not enough for her to be recorded on printed pages. She is recorded in the hearts of the people of Bangladesh.

"One more thing: Gloria looks like a foreigner because of her white skin, but inside she is completely Bangladeshi."

A woman speaks: Sunila Das of Faridpur, the president of the Women's Group of the Bangladesh Baptist Fellowship. Sunila taught 38 years at the Government Girls' High School in Faridpur.

"I met Mrs. Thurman in 1969 when the Thurmans came here to serve the Lord. She started a clinic and she gave medical treatment to Muslims, Hindus, and Christians. She was their mother. When the Thurmans moved to Gopalgonj, the people asked, 'When will our mother come?'

"Mrs. Thurman worked with the little people. She believes all people are equal. She believes that Bangladeshis are equal. She works with us not as an American, but as a Bangladeshi.

"Everyone understands her Bengali. She talks to the village people and they understand her. They believe she is their mother, their sister, their very close friend." Sunila cries softly. "The little boys and girls call her *kaki ma* (father's mother or aunt) or *masi ma* (mother's mother or aunt). They love her very much.

"God sent her to us. We thank God for her."

Another voice from Faridpur is David Rupak Saha, the Rupak whose wedding Gloria helped to arrange. He is an involved member of Faridpur Baptist Church, a lay preacher, and a businessman.

"Missionaries Troy Bennett and Mrs. Bennett were my good friends. They left Faridpur and the Thurmans came. I went with Mr. Thurman to the villages to hand out tracts and Bibles. We were planting seeds. I found the Thurmans really loved the people. They really wanted to preach the Lord's word.

"Then they decided to go to Gopalgonj, a very political place, a very hard place. I told them not to go. Mrs. Thurman told me that there were a lot of people there who need to know the gospel.

"Mrs. Thurman helped to arrange my wedding. Not only does she do that, but she comes and does the dish work at the wedding!"

"Mr. and Mrs. Thurman are no longer just father and mother of Philip and David. They are our father and mother. I love them very much. And Mrs. Thurman, my mother, will be my mother forever!"

An outstanding leader in Bangladesh is Dennis Dilip Datta. For years Dilip was the general secretary of the Bangladesh Baptist Fellowship. He is now general secretary of the National Christian Fellowship of Bangladesh which includes many denominations.

Dilip's friendship with the Thurmans began when they first came to East Pakistan in 1965. Since then, they have worked together in many situations. "I am a product of the Southern Baptist Mission," Dilip says. "I was educated at our seminary in the Philippines.

"In 1974, I went to Faridpur to help after the terrible flood in that area. I stayed with the Thurmans. At two o'clock in the morning, an old Muslim man came and asked Mrs. Thurman to go with him. His daughter-in-law was delivering a baby. In bad weather, in her sari, she walked two miles and helped deliver that baby. I don't believe any other American woman living in a foreign country, in a Muslim dominated society, leaving at that time of the night, walking with an unknown man two miles, would do what Gloria did to help someone. She is exceptional.

"She goes to houses for a meal or a wedding and she helps prepare the food. She peels the vegetables, she washes the dishes. She is a household name in the area. Everyone knows her.

"I have come to their house at midnight and she gets up with a smiling face and prepares food. She washes my clothes. She prepares a good place for me to sleep with my bad back.

"She is our Mother Teresa. She has that kind of concern, that kind of kindness, that kind of love. When there's trouble, she works, she comforts with tears rolling down.

"America should give her the greatest honor. England has the title of Lady. Surely her own country should recognize her greatness."

Ena Chowdhury and her husband, Abdul Muyeed Chowdhury, are very dear friends of the Thurmans. Muyeed is the managing director of Bangladesh Biman, the national airline of Bangladesh. An excellent administrator, Muyeed was deputy commissioner of Faridpur district, then Dhaka district, then commissioner for Chittagong division.

Ena has known Gloria since 1975 when her husband was deputy commissioner in Faridpur. "I met Gloria at a function which was for the care of the needy of the city. I was surprised to find a foreigner wearing a sari in the perfect traditional way. We talked and I found she was a very warm person. I also found she spoke fluent Bengali. That made things quite easy for me. I could be friendly with her. We were at ease with each other and our friendship grew.

"The next year, I had a stillborn baby. I went through many problems, physically and mentally, when I lost my baby. Gloria looked after me. In those days, bread was not available. She would make homemade bread and send it to me. She sent me magazines to read. She did many things for me.

"When I recovered, I visited her home. I discovered she helped not me only. She worked very hard to help many people. She had a clinic. I helped her give out medicine sometimes.

"In Faridpur in those days, we did not have regular electricity. I used to complain, but Gloria never, never complained. It made me think. She is a foreigner and she's not complaining, why should I?

"Gloria had a hysterectomy in Dhaka. People leave our country, especially foreigners, and fly to Bangkok to have surgery. They think we do not have proper facilities, but we do have proper facilities. Even I encouraged Gloria to go to Bangkok. She said, 'Ena, it is all right. There are qualified surgeons here. If anything goes wrong, it could go wrong in Bangkok.' I was so moved by her faith, her trust in God. I find her a very special person.

"I give thanks to God for a good friend like Gloria. She is one of the good gifts God has given me."

Muyeed speaks: "I have known Tom and Gloria nearly two decades now. They are a devoted Christian couple dedicated to their work. On our side, we are a dedicated Muslim family, but we respect each other's religious views.

"Tom is a sober, soft spoken gentleman, a serious worker, a man without pretensions. However, he wouldn't be able to spend so much of his time working without a precious wife like Gloria. She stands by him and does all it takes to live in a place like Gopalgonj.

"We have many sweet memories, like Christmas dinner at the Thurman's home. Another sweet memory we have is when my family and I went to the United States in 1980. I was a Fulbright scholar at the University of Tennessee. Tom had Bob Hall, the Baptist Student Union director meet us at the airport. He transported us and all our baggage to our lodgings. Bob, his wife, Susie, and Mary Hutson took good care of us in Knoxville; it was all because of the concern of Tom Thurman."

James and Dorothy Halder both have shared their love and admiration for the Thurmans. James says, "Sister Gloria is very good in cooking, in serving, and in preaching. She is fluent in Bengali; we never need to correct her. She does so much and whatever she does, she does it with all her heart and soul."

Dorothy claims that Gloria is her example. "I try to raise my son by following her. I try to serve the Lord as she has shown me. I love her very much."

As the Bangladeshis speak, perhaps a fitting conclusion would be the words of Mizan Rashid, who says very simply, "Mrs. Thurman is the first lady of Gopalgonj." Others would add, "And Faridpur. And Dhaka. And all of Bangladesh!"

Simon Sicar, president of the College of Christian Theology of Bangladesh

James, Jose, and Dorothy Halder

Muyeed and Ena Chowdhury and daughters, Sumala and Zirwat

Her Children Arise Up, and Call Her Blessed (Prov. 31:28)

"Our boys are precious, fine young men due in large part to a good mother," Tom says. "When I was gone so much of the time, she carried on. I found that I didn't have to worry. She was capable. When I returned from a three-day trip, I was greeted like I was coming in from a victory march with the Roman Empire! She and the boys were at the gate. It was a wonderful experience.

"We never said to the boys that we believed they were being deprived because they were here. We always told them that God had called us and because He has called us, they were part of it. We also said that we were not saying you are supposed to be doing what we are doing, but for now you are here.

"We don't know in the long run how being born and bred in Bangladesh will affect them, but we do know they have been strong supporters. We are so proud of them."

The pride and love are mutual. Older son, Philip, now a student at Southwestern Baptist Theological Seminary in Fort Worth, Texas, and his wife, Lori, have surrendered to full-time Christian service.

Philip, in a deeply moving discourse, looks at his mother as a mom, a wife, a daughter, a sister, and a friend.

"My mother is able to love when love is nowhere to be found. She is able to give, when there is nothing left to give. She is able to carry on, even when tomorrow looks dark. She is able to heal anything, or so I've always thought! She has the answer to every question. What a teacher, keeping young minds geared in the right direction. She is a constant spiritual leader. When Dad was away she gave us the security blanket of continuing family altar.

"I remember when Mom told me she had leprosy. We were on vacation in Bangalore, India, visiting the leprosy village. As I looked at those disfigured lepers, she said, 'Don't worry. God will take care of me.' That was all I needed to know that it would be all right.

"My mother's dedication to the Lord is complete. Every morning at 4:30 she is at prayer meeting. Every morning, never failing. I'd say to her, 'Why don't you sleep in, Mom?' And she'd say, 'Oh, the mornings are such a blessing.'

"The ultimate servant is a title my mom deserves. She gets up early at home and at the Guest House in Dhaka to make and serve coffee to all her guests. She always thinks of others. She gave her favorite sari to someone who needed it more than she did.

"I think of the sleepless nights she would spend awake because of the pain of arthritis in the neck or hands. The next day, she would pray for strength and work as if no pain was there at all.

"My mother knows how to pray. She takes such heavy burdens to the Lord, wiping the tears as she does. What a heart for people!

"I remember as a worried son asking her to use the car, not to go by local transportation. Her reply was that someone on the bus, the launch, the train needs to know about God. She couldn't risk allowing one soul to perish. I asked if she really had to travel to help with children, youth, and women's camps. She answered that they need to hear. 'If I don't tell them, who will?'

"My mother is the best wife in the world. She is always loyal to God and to her husband. Never did David nor I hear a harsh word spoken between them. There was constant prayer for Dad when he was away. A wonderful meal was placed before him. Fresh clothes were always ready and packed.

"Mom always tries to bring a smile to Dad's face. The unconditional love comes through. I remember praying for their kind of relationship and love in my own life. I thank God that He has given me that in Lori.

"I think of all the times that Dad would bring an unexpected guest for a meal. There was plenty for everyone. She always made the guest feel welcome in our home.

"Gloria Thurman is the best mother in the world. She cared for us and loved us so much. Our pride in her knows no bounds.

"Her work in the clinics is incredible. Mothers came day and night with their sick children. Through the terrified screams of children, her calm voice spoke God's love. At night, someone would come asking for her to come clean a body for burial. She would be gone in ten minutes to share God's love in a grieving home.

"Mom is a loving daughter. She always set aside time to write Bubba, her mother. She would write newsy letters, but she would never tell of the hard times, the pain, the worry. Nor would she ever brag on herself. That is not her way. She would write about David and me. She knew Bubba wanted to hear about us. Her love and concern for Bubba always came through.

"What a sister my mom is, both to her own family and to Dad's. She is always pleased over their accomplishments. I remember how proud she was when her baby brother, Will, went as a journeyman to Kenya. And when Aunt Martha had Amelia, she wept tears of joy! The success of Aunt Jane as an Air Force nurse made Mom so happy.

"Gloria Thurman is a wonderful friend. She feels her friends' heartaches as her own. She grieves with them in their losses of loved ones. She spends hours making cakes to share.

"She became famous for her banana bread. She always puts everybody's needs in front of her own.

"God, help me to be half the person my mother is."

David agrees with all his older brother says. "My mom has to be the greatest mother in the world. I thank God each day for giving me a good Christian mother like Gloria Thurman.

"I remember during the war, Philip and I were outside in the yard at the Guest House in Dhaka. Mom calmly came out and took us in the house. Bombs were falling everywhere, but she behaved in such a way that we were not afraid. I also remember when the war ended, she took an old sari and some scraps and made the new Bangladesh flag. We were so proud of that flag!

"Mom taught me through the tenth grade, except when we were home on furlough and a little while in Woodstock. She put up with a lot from me. In the tenth grade, we both struggled through literature! I left to come to the States to go to school in Tennessee for my junior year. Mom and Dad both had a hard time seeing me go. It was not easy for me, either. But when I left, mom was able to do even more with Woman's Missionary Union. She also was able to become more involved with youth work. She plans the children's camps, and they run smooth as silk. She plans and conducts camps for the youth and women, too.

"Mom has problems with arthritis, but she never complains. It is only by God's grace that she makes it. She goes from 4:30 in the morning until midnight. She works all day long, but she never failed to have time for us. She never complained of being tired.

"I don't know how many trips Mom and I made on the bus to Dhaka. She never complained about the long trips. Usually she was going in because of language school meetings. She is gifted in speaking Bengali. Many of the Nationals ask her to do the translating."

"The villages are a part of my mother's life. She's never had any problem walking countless miles to get to remote places. The people in the villages love and appreciate my parents.

"I am so proud of my mother. I could not ask for better parents."

Wedding portrait: David, Tom, Lori, Philip, and Gloria.

Her Husband Also, and He Praiseth Her (Prov. 31:28)

"Gloria Thurman has the ability to walk with kings and never lose the common touch. She stands to speak and she thrills and blesses the people in Bangladesh," claims Tom. "I'm so proud of her as she speaks fluently and with great power to the people. Yet, she's just as comfortable holding a little mite of a baby covered with sores. Her compassion is genuine, her mercy is of the Lord.

"When I met Gloria," Tom reminisces, "I saw strong character, the ability to handle any situation. I saw a person who gets things done. What I saw was real and true.

"Another thing I noticed about Gloria was her clear sense of God's calling in her life. She has never wavered in this in any way. In the decisions we've made, her call has always been a part of our decision. She has willingly served and she has always become quickly involved in any place we've been.

"I remember when I'd been to Gopalgonj and I went home to tell her I believed God was calling us to Gopalgonj. She said that if I felt that God wanted us to go, she was ready to go. She knew it was going to be difficult. She knew there was poor electricity. She knew we had to go by river launch. But there was never any thought in her mind that we shouldn't go if God was calling us.

"Wherever we've gone, as I've settled in, she has, too. She finds her niche of ministry. She gets involved. When we went to Gopalgonj, within three months she knew most of the children's names. She knew family situations. Even though I had been traveling into Gopalgonj for a long time, she knew more about the ins-and-outs of the community than I had ever known. In this society, women are the go-betweens. So any situation I didn't understand, I would talk to Gloria and she could explain it to me.

"Gloria has always been helpful and supportive. I'd give her a triple *A*+ on her missionary service because of her strong sense of call, her ability to adapt, and her love for the people. Yet during all her missionary outreach, she has been a faithful wife and maintained a consistent home life for our children. I remember many times I saw her in Faridpur when she had her clinic, there might be 50 women and children waiting to be seen by her and her helper. But if Philip or David got a cut or bruise, or if they had a problem or needed something, they called Mom. Gloria always stopped and took time to help them. When they were content, she returned to the clinic. She neglected nothing: not me, not the children, not her missionary duties. And she did each one well.

"God has blessed us as a team. Gloria has the unique ability of keeping on keeping on. Her resilience is amazing. We've had 40 guests in our house and she manages. She cooks, staying up past midnight making angel biscuits for the next morning. Then she's up before daylight for prayer meeting and then preparing breakfast.

"She always surprises us with something special, maybe just something to make the okra or cauliflower taste a little different from the way it tasted yesterday.

"The Mission has called on her to handle many responsibilities. She is presently serving as prayer chairman. She has had a heavy responsibility with language and orientation of new missionaries. In addition, she has been on the national HEED (Health, Education, Economic Development) language board. Any job she accepts, she does well.

"Our teaching and speaking is a strong ministry. In fact, she does as much as I do. Much of her work is in women's work, church camps, and in our local church, Ghosherchar. She's always well prepared and she's always in demand.

"She goes into a home and sits down on that little ten-inch-high stool on the dirt floor of the kitchen. She is sharing their life. They don't think of her as a foreign woman. Often the rest of us are held at arm's length, but not Gloria. She's moved into a different category. As we stay a little longer and our hair gets a little whiter, we become a part of them. Gloria could do most anything now because she is an older, respected, much loved woman. And on her part, if there are onions to be peeled, she peels them. If there are dishes to be washed, she washes them. If there is a Bible lesson to be taught, she teaches it. If there is a dirty child to wash, she bathes him. If there is a leprous man to be cared for, she cares for him. She is always willing to do what she can.

"You read about the baby dying and she wrapped it for burial in a piece of a sheet from our storage barrel. This is the way it is with everything she does. She improvises. I think it's that good, strong Alabama background. She was the oldest child in a family struggling and roughing it. That never hurt anybody. She became a good missionary because of this in her background.

"Another wonderful thing about Gloria is her positive attitude. I try to be positive myself. It's interesting that the Lord has worked it out so that our good days and bad days are at different times, so that we can build each other up. I can remember very few times when we were both on a low level at the same time.

"The Mission says that if we're discussing something that is depressing, I make some remark and help us get 'positive.' Gloria says that's one of my best traits. I think I learned it from her!

"Gloria always looks for beauty and color. It's very easy in this land to become depressed. We made an early decision not to be negative. We promised to tell each other if we became critical. It would be best to go home rather than run the people down.

"We'd be driving along the road and she'd look across the way and see a brilliant green rice field. Then she'd spot a scarlet sari drying on a fence, fluttering in the breeze. She'd say to the boys, 'Look at that bright red sari. Isn't it beautiful against the green of the rice field!' She is always pointing out the beautiful and the good.

"She never complains. I might be upset or even angry, but she never answers in haste. In our bedroom, later, she would tell me how she felt, but never in front of the children, the people, would she reply. She has been a strong, stabilizing force.

"She has never questioned what I felt to be God's will. She would always say that if I was following the Lord, He would have a place for her to serve. And she always found that place, rolled up her sleeves, and went to work. She knows everybody: every man, woman, and child in Gopalgonj and can call many of them by name. She knows whose spleen has been taken out. She is an amazing woman. My decision to marry her was God-given, and He has confirmed it over and over all these years."

Tom says that the well-worn pages and marked verses in her Bible attest to Gloria's spiritual depth. One favorite is Romans 8:28: "And we know that all things work together for good to them that love God, to them who are the called according to his purpose."

Gloria says that this verse grows more precious as she hears James Halder quote it and explain it to those in difficult circumstances in Bangladesh. How beautiful to see good come from bad situations.

Another special verse is Psalm 37:3-5: "Trust in the Lord, and do good; so shalt thou dwell in the land, and verily thou shalt be fed. Delight thyself also in the Lord; and he shall give thee the desires of thine heart. Commit thy way unto the Lord; trust also in him; and he shall bring it to pass."

"These verses were pointed out to me by my Sunday School teacher when I was in the tenth grade," Gloria explains. "They still guide me and mean a great deal to me."

Another is Zechariah 4:6: "Then he answered and spake unto me, saying, This is the word of the Lord unto Zerubbabel, saying, 'Not by might, nor by power, but by my spirit, saith the Lord of hosts.'"

"Especially during the Gulf War crisis and the riots over Salmon Rushdie's book, this verse was precious. God's guardian angel directed the opposition and kept damage to a minimum. Also, during the civil war, when power and might seemed to rage, the Spirit gave us protection and peace.

"Our watchword when we think of leaving at retirement, is 2 Timothy 2:2: "And the things that thou hast heard of me among many witnesses, the same commit thou to faithful men, who shall be able to teach others also."

"This is not only our watchword as we think of leaving, but also a constant reminder of our responsibility," says Gloria.

"Philippians 4:19: 'But my God shall supply all your needs according to his riches in glory by Jesus Christ,' is our family verse. God continues to supply our needs and above. Just recently Philip told us of the church in Lithia Springs, Georgia, voting to give $1,000 a year for Philip's seminary studies. He and Lori had been members there only a couple of months!"

Tom says, "I've often said that God called me to Bangladesh so that Gloria could get here. I have had a lot of respect and honor, but Gloria has had the love of the people wherever we've served."

Empty

The head of the National Christian Fellowship of Bangladesh, Dilip Datta, states, "Jim and Betty McKinley are gone, retired already. By the end of the nineties, R T and Fran Buckley, James and Guinevere Young, and Tom and Gloria Thurman will all retire. Bangladesh will be empty!

"Where are the new missionaries? Where are those who can endure, who have patience, who know how to suffer? Are there none in America like that anymore?"

Are there none? Are we to leave Bangladesh empty of Southern Baptist missionaries?

The Thurmans' story has come full circle, back to the letter written by retiring missionary Rex Ray, the letter that touched Tom's heart as a seminary student. Ray said, "To whom shall I hand the keys? Where are the young evangelists whom God is calling to give their lives of service in preaching the gospel of Jesus Christ to these multitudes who are yet walking in darkness to eternal death?"

In a few years' time Tom and Gloria Thurman will leave their beloved Bangladesh. Their hearts ache with the agony of knowing that no one is coming to Gopalgonj to take their place. There are no missionaries for Faridpur, no missionaries for Comilla, none for Feni, or Chittagong, or Khulna. There is no one for hundreds of villages across Golden Bengal.

Is God suddenly silent concerning Bangladesh? Is He not calling out men and women for the 125,000,000 Bangladeshis?

"Challenge the people to come serve the Lord in Bangladesh," urges Area Evangelist James Halder. "Oh, how we need them, and Bangladesh is not a bad field as the news agents say. Please tell them to come over and help us."

Gloria did not want her story told. "I want the Bangladesh story to be told, but I can't think that one woman's life story will make much of an impact," Gloria argued. "After all, what have I done? Merely lived a day-to-day life in the land to which God has called me. So many others have done likewise.

"Any book about Bangladesh should be written about the men in the Mission. They are the ones who walk many miles, sleep on strange beds, and eat different foods, swallow insults, receive scoldings from Bangladeshis, endure constant separation from families. They take the good news. They witness daily to groups and individuals. They spearhead the church growth."

But Gloria finally relented after much persuasion from Tom and her missionary colleagues.

It was Betty Rains who spearheaded the book. Betty and her husband, Randy, served as Southern Baptist missionaries in Bangladesh. Illness in the family forced their return to the States, but they remain Bangladeshi to the bone. They are praying that God will use this book, *Gloria!*, to call out missionaries to Bangladesh. That is the prayer of everyone who has contributed to make this book possible. And their name is legion!

What about you? What would possess you or anyone to go to Bangladesh? God's call.

What would keep you there? The Thurmans list nine staying forces that have kept them in Bangladesh:

1. God's continuing call
2. The support of the Bangladeshis
3. The positive response of their sons
4. The ability to accept people as they are
5. The desire to see a change in people's lives
6. Faith to believe that God will do what He promises
7. The ability to stay on target, in spite of many side-tracks
8. The ability to look for good in people
9. The desire to spot beauty, even as they travel

Others spot more reasons for the Thurmans' effective service. W. W. Walley of Waynesboro, Mississippi, says, "Tom and Gloria Thurman epitomize what missions is all about as well as any couple I have ever known. I lived in their home when I went to do my little bit in Bangladesh. They love the Lord and the Bangladeshi people. Nothing else could motivate the kind of dedication they show."

Are there none left in America who love the Lord and who feel called to love the millions of people in Bangladesh? Are there none who weep for the children struggling to grow up in Bangladesh?

Are there none who care about the women of Golden Bengal? The Population Crisis Committee graded Bangladesh as 5.5 out of a possible 25 points in quality of health, marriage, education, employment, and social equality of women. This is the lowest life quality of women of any country surveyed.

Is anybody's heart broken for the women of Bangladesh?

Gloria lists victories during the nearly three decades of service there. One victory God has surely ordained is seeing women recognize their worth and desiring to become leaders in the church and the community. What a glorious victory! And there are others:

1. Helping the Bengalis see the need for educating their children
2. Those educated children now taking leadership roles in the church and the society
3. Family relationships developed with the Bangladeshis
4. The happy marriages we've helped arrange
5. Philip and David's willingness to be a part of the team
6. Philip and David's commitment to God and to missions
7. "Savings" concept accepted in household helpers' lives
8. Learning to be optimistic in a pessimistic society

Many people ask Tom and Gloria if the results are worth the risks and the sacrifices and the struggles.

"Look at God's victories, look at lives changed, look at those who will spend eternity in Heaven! Is that worth it? YES!" Tom replies.

Gloria adds, "I'm praying that this book will be God's tool to help young people see how God can take an ordinary life and use it to minister to others—even in difficult places, among stony hearts."

And the Lord said,
"Go ye therefore . . . even to the ends of the earth"
. . . and fifty miles beyond.

Author's note:

As *Gloria!* goes to press, an agriculturalist has been appointed to Bangladesh and is scheduled to arrive in early fall 1993. Also, a family has been approved and is awaiting appointment to Bangladesh. Praise God from whom all blessings flow.

About the author:

Barbara Joiner, the author of *Gloria!*, is pictured on the back cover with Bangladeshi friend, Nripen Boidya. He is holding a stalk of freshly cut bananas from Tom and Gloria's lush tropical garden.

To research *Gloria!*, Barbara spent a month in Bangladesh "following in Gloria's footsteps." She followed from Dhaka to Faridpur to Gopalgonj and into villages like Dattadanga, Hatbaria, and the like. She rode rickshaws, ancient buses, country boats, ferries, and walked many miles—even over bamboo bridges.

"I knew Tom and Gloria were wonderful missionaries. The trip proved they are superlative. I came away awed by their service, their dedication, their love. They make me proud to be a Southern Baptist, and proud to be a supportive, praying WMUer."

Barbara is married to Homer Joiner. They have two daughters, Jackie and Jennifer, and two grandchildren, Megan and Dane. They all live in Columbiana, Alabama.